LIVING ECSTASY

SATYEN RAJA

LIVING ECSTASY

SATYEN RAJA

WarriorSage Inc.

PO Box 12033 • Murrayville RPO
Langley, BC • Canada • V3A 9J5

For more information, visit
www.WarriorSage.com
℃ 1-800-815-1545

ISBN: 978-0-9783206-0-7

Cover and book design by Madison Creative Inc.

Printed in the United States

Dedication

I have been Blessed to have some of the most incredible teachers anyone could dream of having. Some are well known, and some are very private and unknown. They have all served my continuous unfolding in profound ways.

From my fullest Heart I thank Anjali Hill for serving by my side in Awakening. I thank: Lawrence Noyes for his transmission of impeccability; David Deida for his insightful brilliance and for his laser discernment; Stuart Wilde for the wild ride of realizing how to drop spiritual weight; and Aha for his Full Emptiness and for his divine friendship.

Then there are our fabulous, gorgeous, dedicated and gloriously BRIGHT WarriorSage Goddesses who serve along with our valiant, courageous and steadfast WarriorSage Men. They all diligently support my purpose by Serving all of the beautiful students who come to us through the Heart of our WarriorSage offerings. I Love and appreciate you far more than I could ever convey.

This book is only possible and came into existence by the amazingly dedicated work of my divine sister and Editor, Christine Burk. My gratitude and appreciation knows no boundary.

I thank my dearest children, Satori and Shaman, who make sure I really do live up to what I teach, and they keep me clean!

And to my darling self, who is showing up in another body— Suzanne, my Beloved wife. You are the one who inspires me to give of who I am.

I Love you all along with all of those who have served me to serve others.

In humble Gratitude,
Satyen Raja

Contents

continued...

continued...

LIVING ECSTASY

Introduction

Living Ecstasy is the remembering of your birthright. It is your birthright and your true nature to be Ecstatic in the Heart no matter what is going on in your Life. Therein lies the paradox of the call for you to Awaken.

You are probably more likely to pick up this book when you are feeling blue, empty or desperate. While it is true that this book is a wonderful and useful tool that will, through your spontaneous and continuous *practice*, lead you to know the Bliss that permeates all things including your suffering, there is an even more elegant path for you to discover. It is the Path of the WarriorSage within you.

The real gift (and my secret hope) is that you will pick up this book when things are going great for you. Read this book when the abundance of prosperity is brimming over in your spirit. When you embrace this book out of opportunity rather than just out of necessity, you will be able to see that *Living Ecstasy* is the continual revealing of the Ecstasy that is already inherent within you. The Ecstasy that is you is readily available, and it is bursting to be liberated into the world.

All you need to do is to pick up this book and allow your Heart to lead you to the right chapter. Trust. Trust and see what Trust gives you in return when you accept Trust's invitation.

Living Ecstasy is a Mystery waiting to be discovered by you through your own openness and eagerness. The Mystery will unfold through your own excitement to finally Live a Life full of the depth of Happiness. You can finally Live the Life that allows your Joy to know no bounds.

Love and Truth always,
Satyen Raja
May, 2007

— *one* —

HAPPINESS
BRINGS MEANING

"Fringe-dwellers are people who know
there's something else to life other than ego,
tick-tock, control, and the institutions.
Believing and acting differently, they extricate
themselves from common tribal emotions
and make a dash for freedom.
Right now they may still be driving a bus
for the city bus company. But, in their hearts,
they have moved to the outer edge of this
human evolution, beyond what most consider
normal reality. And there are millions of us...
all over the planet, making a difference
to consciousness! Brilliant, really.
The bottom line is, if you are a
fringe-dweller (and you probably are)
and your mind-set doesn't fit,
just agree not to fit."

– Stuart Wilde

YOU DO NOT BELONG

Currently your Life *is a continual quest* to fit in somewhere, to have something or to belong to someone. This predictable pursuit, that is often mislabeled as "finding meaning," is endlessly boring and ultimately unfulfilling. You pour *your PASSION* into this self-important charade as if *that* could *validate* your inconsequential mission. You are either suffering, numb, confused, quietly desperate or faking it.

wake up.

You had it RIGHT from the get-go.
You do not belong.

You search to find meaning in your Life:
> What should I do?
>> What is my purpose?
>>> Who should I have a relationship with?
>>> Why do things happen?
>>>> Why do I feel unsatisfied?

No matter what you get, have or become you *always* want more, need more, seek more.

You. You. You.

You are *seeking* to fill *a lost sense of feeling*.
You *arbitrarily* impose meaning onto your current circumstances.
You go through life randomly assigning meaning to events.
You hope that the results will bring the happiness you lust after.
You feel a sense of displacement.
You feel that you do not fit in.
Deep down, you feel like you do not really completely belong *anywhere*.

The Truth

In actuality you are not placed anywhere. You assume that you are inside something—your body, this room… Yet, you are that which is far Greater. You cannot be confined or defined, so how can you be placed into anything? It is a preconceived notion that has been passed on to you that you are that which is inside your body. Indeed you are that AND much more. You are an Infinite Being; You cannot possibly be defined by something that is confined.

You do not belong. Your feeling of displacement, of not belonging, is the Intuition of your True nature that is waking you up and calling you Home.

The moment you isolate yourself down into one box, you exclude yourself from all other possibilities. That is convenient for living on this Earth plane; however, it has nothing to do with **who you really are**. It is obvious that you do not belong because YOU always ARE.

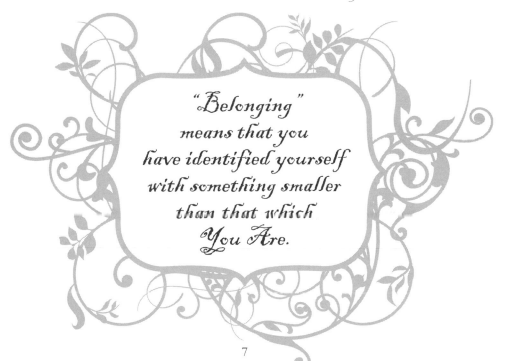

*"Belonging"
means that you
have identified yourself
with something smaller
than that which
You Are.*

Seeking will get you where you already are

Nowhere

No-where

Now-here

You are not located anywhere.
You are that which is far greater.

A Secret

You are what you seek. You are the infinite source of everything (money, sex, power, love & freedom) that you habitually and neurotically seek outside of yourself.

So, Guess What?!

When you search for happiness, the very **source** of your *looking for meaning* **is neurotic seeking itself**. It is the endless cycle of seeking meaning outside of you in order to find joy, contentment or fulfillment. What traps you in this cycle is that whatever you find will be born of seeking to fill a need or to fill a desire. This will *always* end up unfulfilling because if your desire to find meaning comes from lack—which it does—then the fruits of your search will bear the seeds of the lack.

When you are motivated by desire for something you do not feel you have, then even when you do find it, since it came from needy seeking, guess what will happen? You will always end up in disillusionment. The very thing you thought you needed to be happy or to be fulfilled will not hold lasting Bliss or satisfaction but will eventually dissolve.

If the root of your search for meaning comes from emptiness, hollowness, lack or unhappiness, then that is what you will end up with as the result of your seeking.

(CAUTION) You may even think that you are seeking happily from what your Heart desires when in fact you are not coming from your core.

when you come from your True core, you never need seek in the first place.

You are *habitually* unhappy/unfulfilled with a desire to be, at least, content. You *search* for happiness *hoping* that whatever happiness you *achieve* will bring deeper and lasting meaning to your Life. You have it backwards.

If you want happiness, you must

begin with happiness...

Happiness Has Nothing to Do with Your Preferences

how?

How do you "start from happiness?" What does this even mean? Does it mean to do what your first grade teacher taught you to do: Close your eyes and go to your happy place, the place where nobody and nothing can bother you. Where's *that* place? **Where is the place where *nobody can bother you?!*** Where? Where can you go where nothing can touch you or ruffle your feathers?

Happy, dappy, crappy.

Or, for you New Agers: Open and clean all your chakras, so you can surf the cosmic wave of happiness. Nice sentiment, but how has that been working for you when life really hits?

Sit in the Fire

- Do you finally want a solution that works?
- Are you genuinely ready to experience Joy that is sustainable throughout your everyday life?
- Are you so damaged and jaded that even as you read this you are pooh-poohing the possibility of Unreasonable Happiness?
- Would you even accept it if an elegant, truthful, easy solution appeared in front of you?
- Do you need your pain to feel alive?
- Do you have to achieve everything through struggle?

> DO not hide from
> people who can see you.
> ## why?
> BECAUSE they can see you.
>
> DO not hide from
> people who cannot see you.
> ## why?
> BECAUSE they cannot see you.

The Truth

Unreasonable Happiness is REAL. Unreasonable Happiness is your birthright, and it is accessible to you within every moment.

You do have a place within you that is naturally happy without a single reason. This is what Unreasonable Happiness is. Unreasonable Happiness is an inner knowing of unalterable Bliss.

NOTE: UNREASONABLE HAPPINESS IS *NOT* A HAPPINESS THAT DEPENDS ON ANYTHING TRANSITORY SUCH AS WHAT YOU DO OR DO NOT HAVE. IT IS NOT BASED ON A "BECAUSE." YOU ARE NOT HAPPY BECAUSE THIS HAPPENED OR BECAUSE SHE FULFILLED YOUR NEEDS OR BECAUSE HE TOOK CARE OF BUSINESS. YOU COULD FALL IN LOVE, GET A PROMOTION AND WIN THE LOTTERY ALL IN ONE DAY, YET YEARS LATER FEEL LIKE CRAP BECAUSE YOU LOST IT ALL, WASTED IT ALL OR SPENT IT ALL.

Unreasonable Happiness is not sourced in anything.

Unreasonable Happiness has nothing to do with your needs, desires or preferences being met.

Your core happiness is sourced from a place that is in no way connected to your preferences.

The infinite well of
unreasonable Happiness
springs eternally
from your own
true nature.

The Money Question

Are you willing to curb the incessant gorging of your
preferences to surrender to the actual Source of
Eternal Bliss that is this moment waiting to Live you?

The Bottom Line

The fulfillment of your personal needs and preferences
is not how you tap the unlimited well of Unreasonable
Happiness within you.

START WITH HAPPINESS
AGAIN AND AGAIN

Is Unreasonable Happiness *really* already within you?

It is within you, and it is shiny and yearning to be evoked. When you Live your Life with an OPEN HEART, and you give your gifts, then you are offering the part of you that is untouchably HAPPY.

DO IT NOW. Intuit the part of you that is already Free. Offer that to the world. **As best you can, simply emanate Love in all directions.**

Inherent in offering—Good work, Good intentions and Good actions—is meaning. When you offer, you automatically come from fullness. You intuit the part within you that is already Free, and you offer that. **Rather than seeking happiness, transmit happiness.** Cease your searching for meaning from a place of emptiness or from a place of lack.

Begin to serve the world as the Unreasonable Happiness and the fullness that *you already are*.

Your innocence is gone. Unreasonable Happiness is your choice. From now on, you can always get to your own Unreasonable Happiness. The fastest foolproof way is to give with an open Heart to another whatever it is that you yourself want or need, without waiting. More later...

When you start to offer happiness in the moment AS YOU ARE a miracle will happen. A depth of meaning, which has so far often eluded you, will magically enter the circumstances and the relationships of your Life.

This discovery may inspire you.
You will probably become even more curious
about the purpose of your Life and
your next steps
in the world.

The crucial difference is that you will be finding the answers from the place in you that is **already** unalterably HAPPY, unfailingly **LOVED** and absolutely **FREE**.

What will bloom is HAPPINESS itself because the seeds of this search are the seeds of HAPPINESS. What blooms is LOVE if the seed is LOVE (a hint for how to have the relationship of your deepest longing). What blooms is FREEDOM if the seed is FREEDOM.

{In kind, if the seed is tension, then the fruits will be of tension. If the seed is the desperate seed of lack, you will end up with the fruits of lack.}

CAUTION

Do not get lost in the idea that once you find Meaning/Happiness that you are done, and you will always be happy.

If you do this, you are removing your happiness by shelving it into a future condition.

This is a trap.

You are shelving your fulfillment for later: when you find meaning, then you will be happy...

Moment-to-moment come freshly from the place within you that is already HAPPY.

UNREASONABLE HAPPINESS

Relax. Feel within you, the part of you that is already Happy, already Free, already Love. **The meaning in your Life actually flows from this limitless well.** How could you offer that out into the world to your friends, to your family, to your colleagues and even to strangers, in a way that would **bring more meaning to their lives**?

When you practice opening from the place of Fullness, Freedom and Love when you do not feel it to be so. . . then the greatest gains are made.

When you are angry at your lover, you are sure that you are in the right, and you are feeling the sting and closure of your hurt and fury—this is the ideal time to PRACTICE. From *this* place and in *this* moment intuit the part of you that is already Free and transmit *that*.

What would it look like to offer that instead? What could happen if you were to give to your Lover while touching your own inner Wisdom and Joy? What if you offered genuine Bliss no matter what else is going on?

In whatever conditions you find yourself, offer meaning to the world by coming again and again from the inexhaustible well of Unreasonable Happiness within you.

infect the world with your Bliss.

REMEMBER YOUR HEART

Do you know the Legend of Atlantis?

*Of course, the story of Atlantis has many tellings…
that is why it is indeed a Legend.*

One of the legends of Atlantis goes like this… The people of Atlantis cultivated and deeply raised their consciousness.

In fact, just prior to the beginning of the legend, the first real Initiates into this Earth realm, a group of beings with high Awareness decided that this pretty blue planet looked quite interesting. Before you knew it, a group of them had squeezed through from the expansiveness of where they were to the dense location of *this* incredible place. Some people called this place *Mu*, others called it *Atlantis*.

With much work and experience, the beings of Atlantis raised their Awareness to Crystalline Consciousness. The people raised a particular spectrum of their consciousness to a higher realm, and they vibrated there. They rose quickly to great heights… But, guess what they forgot? They forgot their Heart.

They forgot the **simplicity of their humanity**.

That is how the legend goes…

It is sort of like what is happening right now with technology. Currently, there is an incredible capacity for innovation, but unless *you* keep including the Heart up-to-pace with the technology, in Reality, *the Heart will lose its sacredness*. By the sheer nature of the force of that energetic phenomenon, everything will eventually self-destruct. It has to.

———

There are many alternative realms with higher energies,
healing energies, vibratory states of consciousness that
many of you often enter through different means: yoga,
meditation, drugs, breath, intention and growth-work.

The challenge arises when you raise (or lower)
your vibration to experience another realm,
but you forget to consciously include your Heart.

You may enter another state of Awareness bodily or
mentally, but you may not *intentionally* OPEN YOUR HEART.

The Heart does not need to raise its vibration;
It is you who chooses to open and include It.

The Heart is Existence, and It *is* outside
of all conditions; it cannot be lowered or raised.

The Heart sees each and every person
as the perfection of Existence.

The Heart does not raise your vibration nor its own.

The Heart simply shows what is.

If you over-associate with vibration,
you will become a **vibration junkie**.

You will spend your Life obsessed with trying
to continually raise the vibration.

This is wasteful.

———

There is no point to being in any place, state or realm without the Heart, YOUR HEART. Open your Heart.

- 🖤 Remember your Heart throughout every day and throughout all of life.
- 🖤 No matter how transcendental you get, if you forget the Heart you will walk around in transcendental existences that you *think* are Truth.
- 🖤 **Truth** is when all existences are *removed*.
- 🖤 In **Truth** there are no higher or lower spheres, realms or states.
- 🖤 Any sense of higher or lower is part of the Illusion.

When you simply Love another, is that not enough?

When you feel fully Loved, is that not enough?

Is that not a moment of true depth?

Give your Heart for the sake of others

Atlantis went down because it was going too high. Existence maintains perfect balance, and the Universe will always provide the opposite to correct. **This is the legend: Atlantis sunk into the sea. Why? Because it rose too high without consciously including the Heart.** Your job is to learn from these metaphors; whether they are real or not is irrelevant. There is a legend in there…

The
Legend
Is
You.

— *two* —

YOUR BIGGEST KINKS ARE YOUR GREATEST GIFTS

"self-improvement is better than shame but less
mature than openness... you can't help but live
true to what is, whatever is. you stop trying to
buoy yourself with motivation and positive
thinking. you open as the lack and the darkness
you sometimes feel. you are willing to feel,
breathe, and be everything, dark and light.
opening in every now-moment, your life is no
longer lived as hope for success and love, but
as an unfolding openness... if you are willing to
feel exactly what is and open as you are, then
your life unfolds as truth. for instance, if you
feel you are nothing, then open as nothing,
fully... every moment, no matter how bad or
good, is unfolding open. the hope for personal
success and positive emotion is most fascinating
when you have forgotten, or have yet to
discover, the endless opening you are."

– david deida

KINKS

You have kinks: you have parts of you that shut down due to old conditioning when you are stressed and when things get stirred up in your soul. A kink occurs when you feel that the Freedom that is inherent in your nature is contracted; you are caught up in your own troubles, your own sorrows and your own sadnesses. The difficulty that you feel when your Heart is not flowing as fully as it could be is pain, fear or tightness that is resulting from your kinks. Kinks are the energetic crooks twists and bends that occur in all levels of your being: in your mind, in your body and in your emotions.

A kinky kink

Say, for example, that when you were a child, you used to play by hiding in the coat closet for fun. One day while hiding, you accidentally hear your older brother and his girlfriend start to make out in the TV room near you. A rush of sexual energy hits you and BAM! For the rest of your life, you now have a kink which is that the smell and feel of leather in the dark turns you on.

Imagine a water hose, turn on the tap. The water will naturally flow. If you crimp the hose, the water cannot flow as Freely. Like the bent hose, you have too much pressure up to the point of the bend in the hose and not enough pressure after the point of the bend in the hose. The whole system locks up. Energetically, Asian medical traditions have known about this for thousands of years through the study of disciplines such as acupuncture. The yogis have known it through the nadis in the body. Modern psychology calls this phenomenon the "shadow self" or unconscious barriers. Whatever the tradition, kinks happen in all levels of your being: in your mind, in your body and in your emotions.

So, Guess What?!

Some part of you is *sick* and *tired* of your own stuff: your history, your problems, your accumulated burdens. The unconscious conditioning that you picked up as a child, all the unhelpful and unsupportive habits you learned from society, parents, upbringing and all early harmful influences, are the accumulated kinks which crimp, bind and lock down the Free flow of the inherent Freedom of your Being.

Everyone,
including you,
has these so-called kinks
in their consciousness
that restrict the
Free flow of
the Heart.

You can see kinks in others quite clearly; in fact, **it is very easy to see everyone else's kinks.** That is the humor of Life. It is simple to see where other people are screwed up, or where they are not Living their Life from their fullest expression.

(CAUTION) When you are focusing on where others lack, you are actually living from your own kinks, the unconscious habits that shut you down from

your own magnificence.

YOU WILL NEVER
OVERCOME YOUR KINKS

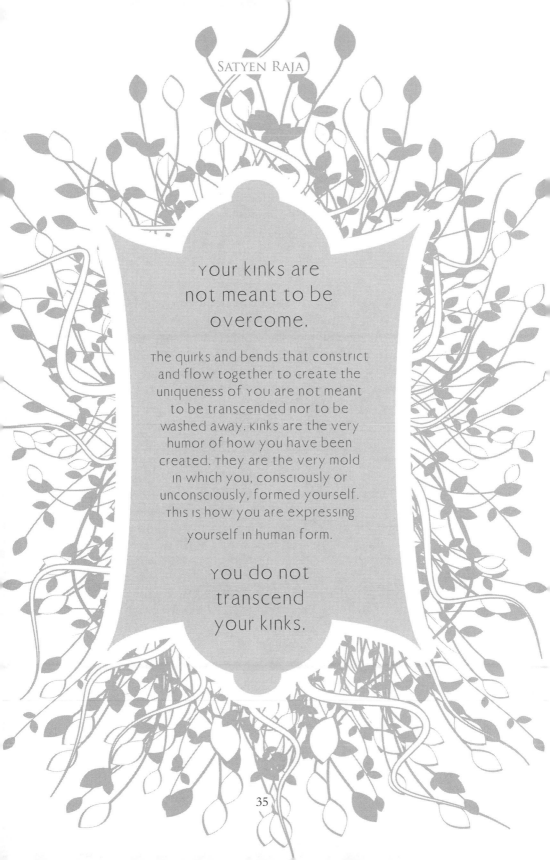

Your kinks are
not meant to be
overcome.

The quirks and bends that constrict
and flow together to create the
uniqueness of you are not meant
to be transcended nor to be
washed away. Kinks are the very
humor of how you have been
created. They are the very mold
in which you, consciously or
unconsciously, formed yourself.
This is how you are expressing
yourself in human form.

You do not
transcend
your kinks.

There are many strategies to try to overcome your kinks, to fix them, to unblock them, to move them or to therapize them out of existence. When you have done work on yourself long enough, you tend to think that you have cleared out, risen above or let go of some of your kinks. However, when a stressful situation, that triggers an old pattern, arises all of a sudden your kinks come flooding back to the surface. You think, "No! I thought I had evolved passed that."

your kinks are part of you forever.

When kinks are non-illuminated; when they are not *shining* with the wisdom of the Awakened Heart; when they are not glistening with the profundity of the inherent depth of your Being, then your kinks become aberrations. Instead of simply being how you experience the flow of Life, your kinks become the cramped restriction of that flow which keeps you from *remembering* Who You really Are and limits your behavior down into tightened, predictable patterns.

However, when your inner Light shines from your Open Heart, then your kinks literally become Illuminated. Your own *pristine* life force runs through your kinks. Instead of impeded flow, the immaculate humor and creativity of your core being are naturally released. Through awareness—which is simply your conscious choice to open your Heart under any condition—kinks become art, the art that is your Life. Your kinks become the way you express your full nature. Your kinks are the art form through which you give your gifts to the world.

The Truth

Your kinks are not actually something that limit, confine or imprison you. Your unique kinks are what create the brilliant one-of-a-kind expression of you in this world. You are that which can never be imprisoned or limited. You are that which has never been nor ever can be confined. The part of you that thinks you have been restricted is simply the mechanism of how you imagine yourself to be limited, so that you have an individual identity. Your kinks provide this identity. It is literally how you know that there is a unique and separate "you."

Accept

The advice to "accept yourself as you are" is so often and casually used that the power of this simple Truth is watered down, overlooked and under-used. The first step to use your Life force to create art out of your life rather than for the suffering you are currently so attached to, is to accept your kinks. In order to do this do not rely on therapy alone. Do not wallow in the misery of how you accumulated your kinks. Your kinks are many: parents, family, money, abundance, sex, success, power, food, self-worth, beliefs, neuroses, preferences, behaviors... Whatever happened when you were little that gave you the idea that you are limited in some way is your kink in that area. Accept yourself as you are. Acceptance means letting your kinks Be...without the hostile, New-Age idea of cranking them out of existence. Your kinks are not a problem, so stop making them one. **Stop making your kinks a problem.**

To truly accept yourself, kinks included, means to rest softly within the warmness of your Heart knowing that somehow your history has formed you this way. You do not know why. You do not need to understand your kinks. You do not need to label them as good or bad, useful or destructive. You are just resting in the eternity of, "I am who I am. So be it." Accept at a core level that you are never going to be fixed, and that you are never going to be cured. There is actually no cure to seek. There is a resting and a humble reckoning of all the shit and Light that makes up your personality.

That is the first step: accept yourself. Your kinks are never going to go away. Do it right now. Put your hands over your Heart. Just accept: "I am who I am with all my inherent tendencies; with all the upbringing that I received from my mother, from my father and from society. I received all of that. I liked some of it. I did not like some of it." Gently touch your body with the tacit, tactile offering of acceptance. Acknowledge your own being simply as the way it is in this moment.

LOVE

The next step of making art out of your Life is to Love deeply your very own Being. Love what you have accepted. Soften your Heart to your whole family, to your own being, to your own history, to your ideas and to your own opinions.

You can soften your Heart simply by intending it. Soften the self-judgments of your own endless, exhausting efforts to overcome your kinks. Just love yourself. Wrap your arms around your whole being, your whole head, your whole body. Give yourself the deepest hug that anyone has ever given you. Know that this Love is for you, and it is coming right from you. Become your own Lover. See yourself as an imperfect Lover that is being enraptured, uplifted and beloved by another imperfect Lover. Only imperfect Lovers can truly Love each other. What is Love without seeing and Loving through the imperfections of another?

The very act of Love requires that there is something on the other side that you might think may not deserve the fullness of Love. Love yourself anyway. Move beyond the peace of acceptance and into the Heart warming shine of Love. "I Love myself, as I am, as I am created, with all my history, with everything I have walked through and with everything I walk towards; I Love myself." **Do it boldly. Do it bodily. Treat yourself well.** Pamper yourself. Love yourself.

> *Without needing a single change in any circumstance or condition choose to Love yourself right now. Even if you don't feel it, choose to love yourself anyway.*

You intuitively already know how. Find the courage to Love yourself deeply with all your inherent kinks, and then you will be ready for the hidden key to prosperity, the next step, which is to Bless.

BLESS

Find the saint within you

When a saint sees others who are struggling, the saint does not condemn, condone, judge, harass, demand or whip them into shape. A saint offers Blessing, and Blessing is a force. It is a force of thunderous softness. It is a force of divine okay-ness. Blessing is a transmission of gentleness. Within you there already exists a living saint, and that saint has the capacity to Bless. Be still and feel the part of you that perpetually exists as an untarnished Blessing. Know the part of you that is a saint.

You are a living Blessing.

The very fact that you are in existence is a Blessing force upon all beings in all times, in all places and in all dimensions.

It is the case.

So, with your own hands, as if your hands are the hands of a saint, Bless your history. Bless your family of origin and all of its kinks. Feel in your soul that you are pouring Blessing force through your Heart, through your palms, through your whole being on to your past and on to all the factors that have shaped you—good, bad and indifferent. Bless your own body—this vessel of co-creation, this vessel of relationship that you have with yourself, others, nature and the whole Universe. Bless every part of you that you wish to hide, that you do not wish to show. Bless whatever you have shame around. **Deeply from the saint within you, Bless yourself.** Allow yourself to be touched and affected by this Blessing.

As the warmth of Blessing washes through you, press it out in all directions for all to gain.

ACCEPT, LOVE, BLESS & MAKE ART OF YOUR KINKS

When you look at people, such as great comedians, who have had all types of weird, strange conditionings to form them into who they are, notice that these are not balanced, normal people. These are people whose lives have been damaged in irrevocable ways. What they have done is accept, Love and Bless their weirdnesses. They have turned their aberrations and unusual attributes into some expression that makes art which brings through the Freedom of pure spirit. Through their kinks, with their kinks, *they utilize their wackiness.* They employ their quirky attitudes, their strange postures, their unresolved family dynamics, and they find the humor in it all. Most importantly, *they then share that with the world.*

To make art means to uplift other people with the bizarre and wonderful compilation that is you. Contribute to the world at large through your kinks, not by trying to get rid of them, but by **gracefully accepting, Loving and Blessing your strangeness, your brokenness and your history**. Bring Freedom and Love out through others by opening their Hearts with the divine display of your foibles. Make it your mission to bring their deepest smiles to the surface. There is a certain mystery of what it will look like for you, but know that you cannot get it wrong. Great athletes have done it; great martial artists have done it. Great poets and musicians have taken their pain and suffering, and they have made such music out of it. Artists make drawings that come from the uniqueness of the crimps in their psyche. All types of kinks reveal endless dimensions that make people, "Ooohl and Aaah!" and open up into realms that they can then feel and experience within themselves.

A Secret

Make
art
out of
your
kinks.

That
is the
secret.

GIVE IT ALL AWAY!

This is your heroic journey,
to learn cunningly and with humor
how to make art out of your own kinks.

Remember to start by
Accepting,
Loving and then
Blessing them.

A key to Ecstasy is that once you have
discovered *how*, even one little way, to
make art out of your kinks,
do not hold back!

Give fully.

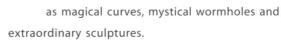

Throw your whole Life into your Heart and
let your Heart pour through your kinks,
so that your kinks shine through
as magical curves, mystical wormholes and
extraordinary sculptures.
Become a Living art, become a Living art,
become a Living art in this Life.

And Bless all beings.

Expand!

To begin, wholeheartedly intend to do just one of these steps as earnestly as you can. This is enough to begin. **Invite Grace to enter.** Once you practice this, you will gain momentum with more fluidity, more relaxation and more artistry, then offer that to all other beings! *See* everyone else; look for their kinks. Do not try to hide, and playfully do not allow others to hide. Do not just look for the good in others. See all of their natures—their light to their dark—and accept it all. In the same way you gave to yourself, accept all others' kinks. Love their kinks. Love *them*. The way you can do that is to feel your Heart. Your Heart is like a deep, warm radiant sun. Through your Heart you are shining. **Shine your Heart deeply into their kinks,** their strangeness, their closures and their habits. Pour in that sun force of your Loving Heart. Let it warm and soften the shells of their kinks, and then Bless them from the saint within you. **Bless their whole Being**: their light to dark, their obstructions, their talents, their history, their family tree. Bless them, so that they are released into the future and into the present. Lovingly and artfully show them how you are making art of your kinks, so they can transform their kinks into art as well.

The legacy of our collective sum of experiences from amazing to mundane is our whole legacy. Our shared job is to make art out of it all.

Find the art in others,
so that we all become the
Living dance that is our
inherent right, the real
meaning of Free will and
our True nature.

NO ONE NEEDS TO
TEACH YOU ANYTHING

Close your eyes. Feel to the origin of your birth. For magical, mysterious and unknown reasons you became incarnated into your particular family. From your deepest Heart, widen. You do not have to like the conditioning and all of the aspects in which you were brought-up, but in this moment you can accept it, Love it and then from the Divine in you, Bless it. It has all brought you to this moment. Bless it wide. You do not have to like any of it, just Bless it. Feel all the forces of closure, suffering, pain and yearning that have molded you into who you are. Growing up as a child, what molded you into a teenager forming who you hung out with and who you did not? Bless all of that, too. Bless who you dated and had relationships with. It formed you, and it evolved you.

You are a Warrior. You are a saint. You are a Sage. Make art out of the kinks that form your Being.

What to Do?

As a wide-open being, you pressed through a narrow tube of Life, and were molded, so that you could be birthed into this moment now. All of those pinches, crimps, suffering, hurts and historical experiences have allowed you to become the artist formerly known as your history. When you open your eyes, you will be born Blessed with your history. Your history is the Blessing force that is incarnating you in this moment. You do not have to get rid of your kinks, you just have to learn to open *as* them and give whatever you are *without holding back*.

— three —

FILL THE ROOM
WITH WHO YOU ARE

"I have found the paradox
that if I love until it hurts,
then there is no hurt."

— MOTHER TERESA

The World Needs You

Whether you know it or not, the world needs you. The world needs all your gifts, all your Love, all your spirit and all your body. The world urgently needs all of you. The world is yearning for you to fall into union with it. The world itself is beckoning you to fill it with your unreserved presence and with your radiant Love. The world is beckoning you to give all of your unique talents, gifts and capacities without hesitation and without reservation. The world needs all of your brokenness, all of your smallness and all of your shyness. The world is the great room, the great mansion: my Lord's mansion has many rooms.

This is a room. Wherever you show up, is the room you are in whether it is a car, a bathroom, your job, your relationship, a thought, a field, an ocean or a state of consciousness. Wherever you find yourself is the room. Fill the room with who you are: this is your service to your Loved ones and to the Universe. What this practically means is that you give of yourself without holding back to the space around you, even if there is no one around you. Give of yourself even if you think it is ridiculous, meaningless, unimportant or insignificant.

You are always in relationship to everyone even though they may not be in the room with you. They could be on the other side of the planet, yet you are still in relationship with them. They are over there. If you do not know that they are there, it does not matter. They are there. When you fill up the room with you, even when you are alone in an empty room, you do the world a service. You serve humanity by offering the emanations of your fullness, your richness and your liberation. This is felt, and it is transmitted. **Your offering is a profound gift to all beings.**

When you are not filling the room with who you are, it is because you are believing some imagined limitation of yourself. You have these ideas that you are less than what you are: "I am broken; I am poor, I am miserable; my relationships are not working; I am not enough." Such thoughts and beliefs contract your infinity down into a small, burned-out, washed-out and decrepit version of your True self. You contract down. It is literally an action. The action is performed again and again. Part of you has not yet woken up and realized that you yourself actually are Love and Freedom rather than a broken being who is incessantly trying to *get* Love and Freedom.

The Futility of Seeking Love through Pleasure and Freedom from Constraint

AS your true nature you are Love and you are Freedom.

When you forget that, you seek erotic ways to fill yourself with Love by trying to fill yourself with pleasures that are outside of you. You seek pleasure through food, pleasure through sex, pleasure through TV, pleasure through shopping and pleasure through drugs. You continuously seek to fill an empty void that can never be filled because it can never be filled. It goes on and on, and the void is always empty at the bottom. You try to fill it and to fill it with waning pleasures that you hope will lead to Love.

when you are not seeking to be filled with Love, you are trying to break out of some constraint and into Freedom. You try to break away from the bills and the mortgage. You try to break out from the stress of your relationship; from the soreness of your knees; from the curse of disease; and from the pressures of your job. You neurotically try to break Free from something and into something else that you hope will give you more Freedom.

When you start to wake up, rather than incessantly trying to fill yourself or continuing to break out of some so-called lack, you just say: "I am going to walk in and fill the room with who I am, as I am, now." Fill it! You do not need to be full to fill the room with you. You need to fill the room, and then you will be filled. You do not need to be full of Love and Freedom to fill the room. When you fill the room with *who you are*, you are now Free to Love. When you fill the room, you are the Living embodiment of Freedom. When you fill the room, you are the Living embodiment of Love.

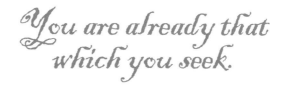

You are already that which you seek.

YOUR MOST NATURAL STATE

what does it really mean to fill the room
with who you are?

what does this look like?

HOW is this relevant or practical
for your life?

Consider this true story...

A woman at the embittered end of a broken relationship was embroiled in a nasty custody battle over her children. She was so tired and angry at her ex that she literally felt like she could find nothing in him that was left to Love. Their battle was fierce, yet he had far more money and resources than she had. Her Heart grew weary with fear and hate. The woman knew that she was probably going to lose the custody battle.

Suffering, broken and exhausted the woman decided to try to find some redeeming quality in the man she had once been in Love with. She tried and tried, but she was filled with bad memories and venom, and she could find nothing. Finally, she remembered something. Each and every morning when making the children's lunches, the man had taken great care to cut up little pickles and neatly arrange them on each sandwich. He did this with such genuine care that it warmed her Heart a little even to remember it.

By the time the day of court arrived, the woman had somehow transformed. She was soft and open. She had been intentionally focusing on the single Loving act that this man had daily made for their children with the pickles. She was extremely sad that she would probably lose the court battle, and she was still willing to do whatever it might take to have custody of her children. At the same time, she was rested in her Heart.

Court looked like it was going to turn out as she had dreaded. Yet she allowed the softness to remain in her Being. She openly permitted all of the fear and pain to course through her as she purposefully continued to focus on the pickles—the one aspect she knew she could genuinely Love in this man. At the very last moment before the judge was about to end the case by giving custody to the man, the man suddenly turned to the woman and dropped the case entirely. After endless days of hostility and rage, at the shocking moment when the man was sure to win, he simply said that they would find a way to share custody somehow.

At your core, in your most natural state you are Freedom and you are Love. To fill the room with who you are, means to offer Love and Freedom in whatever emotional state you are in or whatever conditions you find in the room. You offer Love and Freedom regardless of the outcome or of any consequence. The woman could only give Love through her own pain by focusing on the gesture of the pickles. That was her filling the room with her true and Loving essence. As an added miracle, the man also filled the room with his True and Loving essence.

A Secret

The secret teaching is that when
you to seek to give by filling the
room with who you are, you end
your own seeking and you fulfill your
true purpose. The greater secret is
that this is the way to draw to you
what it is you seek: you give it. The
trick is you do not give it because
you want to get it. You give it
because that is how you fill the
room with who you are, which is,
ultimately, the only real reason
you are here.

There Is Nothing Else to Do

What to Do?

Put your attention on the room
that you are in right now.

Feel your body.

Feel how you are sitting.

Notice your breath.

Just feel that.

Begin to feel your space in the room,

what space are you occupying?

Feel how small it is compared to the room.

NOW,

*imagine your consciousness
is inside your body,*

that YOU are looking through your eyes and
through your soul out at the room.

Imagine that your consciousness is
inside your body,
and look out from that place.

You can see things are separate from you.

You are taking up this little corner of the universe, called "I,"

in the body

in the room

looking out.

NOTICE:

How small do you feel?

At this moment how much Love is in your Heart?

Become Aware of what feelings of contribution
you have, being in this isolated, dense package.

Observe how Free you feel.

What extent of Freedom do you have?

Do you have some?

You can move around. You can get yourself a glass of
water or something to eat. You do have some Freedom.

Start breathing deeper, and begin
straightening and expanding your spine.

Feel your spine rising to the ceiling.

Feel that your hips are open wide;

the whole front of your body is softening.

The whole front of your face is softening.

Your breath is

deepening and
widening.

continued...

Your Awareness is now not just in your body,
but it is moving out a few feet into the space around you.
Feel that the space around you is you, and it is getting
bigger and bigger. Feel whatever feelings are happening
in your body. Simply notice your thoughts and feel
your feelings whatever they may be.

Fill the room with your
presence and radiance.

If your body starts to open and to expand in some way,
let that happen. You may find your breath deepens,
your posture becomes even more expressively wide
or your chest expands. Let it happen.

Fill every corner of the room with your presence.

Fill up the space with you as if the whole room is Living.
The room *is* the Living you.

Now how full do you feel?

Do you feel like you have to fill yourself up with something outside
of you, or do you feel like offering your own fullness outwardly?
Do you feel like you are neurotically trapped in some cage
that you need to scratch your way out of?
Or are you already Free to be in the room,
so that you can offer your intrinsic nature?

Eventually, you will consciously do this because
there is nothing else to do.

Fill the room.

If you are in a large room,
fill the whole room.

There is no end to the capacity of the room
or to the bounty of you.

YOUR AURA IS NOT A CONSTRAINT

The aura is not a limitation. Your aura is a field of contractions upon subtler contractions. You do not need to expend any time or any energy worrying about your aura. The very act of trying to protect a barrier around you announces to the Universe that you are something that needs protecting.

Your aura is an energetic field that maintains your physical body. As long as you are not indulging in abusing yourself... As long as you are shining your naked Heart as best you can, be at Peace that you are the whole within the whole.

Sit in the Fire

The Infinite Self is wider than all auras put together. Your Infinite Self is the nature of all existence. There is no end. There is no barrier of separation. Ultimately, filling the room with who you are is to fill the Universe with the Awareness of Self. Your True Self is absolutely wide and endlessly bountiful. Your Infinite Self is without end and without beginning. To emanate that— whether you *know* it or not—is to offer the fullest expression of yourself to the room.

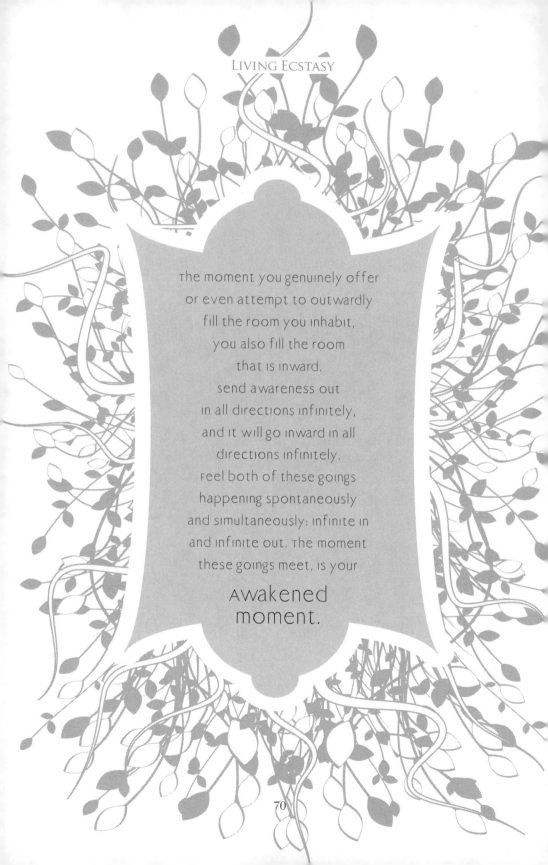

The moment you genuinely offer
or even attempt to outwardly
fill the room you inhabit,
you also fill the room
that is inward.
Send awareness out
in all directions infinitely,
and it will go inward in all
directions infinitely.
Feel both of these goings
happening spontaneously
and simultaneously: infinite in
and infinite out. The moment
these goings meet, is your

Awakened
moment.

You Are the Source

?

What does it mean to be the source of all things? What if the Truth of this reality could penetrate your body? **You are the source of all things.** What if your entire Life was Lived from this knowledge? What if you made all of your decisions from this foundation rather than from the lack, need or limitation that you currently use as your source?

Whatever emotional state you are in, you do not need to change it. Simply choose to open in the moment as that, whatever that may be. As you are, feel and offer yourself infinitely outward and infinitely inward at the same time. As you perform this profound meditation you are the center point. Offer yourself as a gift. Let go of expecting or needing anything in return. Do it as a practice. Infinitely in…and infinitely out…feeling…expanding…*offering*.

What to Do?

Whenever you feel that Life is too much or that you do not have enough, immediately practice filling the whole room infinitely with Who You Are. At the same time fill the whole room infinitely inward. Know that if you are infinite in all directions, then you are always the center of the Universe. Whenever you are feeling Infinity in all directions, the whole Universe revolves around you.

There is no need to grab from smallness because you know that everything is already yours. Infinity in all directions means that you are literally and consciously at the center of it all. While doing that practice, you have nothing to do but to give Love and to give Freedom. At that moment you are unburdened from your mind. You have no need to fret over the condition of your aura or of anything else. At that moment, you are released of your personal history and of your karma. You release everyone else's karma.

Awaken so that Others May Awaken

Filling the room with who you are is a practical gift to other people. Other people want your Love. They want your Life force. They want your vivaciousness. They want to hear about your dreams and about your passions. Even if the world does not want to hear, offer it anyway. In the deepest Hearts of EVERYONE, they all want to hear.

Everyone wants to touch Bliss.
You have an infinite supply. Give it away.

Ultimately, filling the room with who you are ends up in the recognition that you are the room of all that is, you are the absolute room. Inclusively you are the room that confines and is confined. Expansively you are the room that exists in boundless space. When you are identified to an "I am," you are the room. When you experience yourself without a point of referential "I," then you just are room for all things to Be. When the last vestige of "I" is let go, then there is just room. The nature of existence is service. You are either aware of this or you are not. When you fill the room with who you are you bring the Love and Freedom that is inherent in yourself and in others to the world.

(CAUTION) Fill the room with who you are. Feel, are you doing that right now? If you are not, then you are not merely withholding your gifts and your Blessings from others. You are creating suffering. The very act of holding is what perpetuates suffering, including your own. If all you can offer in this moment is that you feel stuck, then offer that. Any feeling you offer fully through your open Heart is the gift of you that you have to give. Any intentional offering whatsoever will decrease suffering and increase Ecstasy. Take the very thing you are resisting, and give it as an offering. Do it now. Give yourself to the room now.

So, Guess What?!

When you fill the room with who you are, guess what happens to others? Either they shrink more into their cages because the bright openness of your expansion sheds Light on and magnifies their closures, their case, their self-importance, their indulgence, their laziness or their self-worth; or, they are drawn out into the Light because of their hunger for real contact. If **you give yourself to the room, you can spark the Awakening in others**. Their breath and their bodies will fill until they too spill out into the room in fullness.

They will
expand,
brighten
and Lighten.

They will be less tuned in to the mechanistic mind-set. They will be less caught up in the machinations of their never-ending ego.

Enlightenment is the embodied
living expression of illumination.

Enlightenment can happen two ways: as a spontaneous shift or as a slow unfolding. Your responsibility is to actively practice giving yourself, your Light, to the room regardless of the conditions or of the results.

when you offer your Light
by intentionally filling the room with it,
you illuminate the whole world.

— four —

OPEN UNDER
ANY CONDITION

opening in the midst of any condition:
a practice from Aha

"it is important to realize that all conditions
themselves that can be noticed over and
against oneself occur within the limitless light
that is the greater condition of the REAL.

this means that any event to be noticed
and reacted to has its genuine context
in a BEING-ness that is void of expectations
or picking sides.

consider that your own restricted movement
of body/mind, breath/feeling attention is
the cause of seeing the greater limitless
condition modified as the present
circumstances that bind you to an attitude
of any kind, positive or negative.

To live as the openness that is one's real
nature, the very condition that is infinity,
is to cultivate perfect acceptance of the
conditions you are passing through including
all reactions that you would like to open past.

In such moments make the choice to breathe
in the nourishment of the situation which
one exists through and feel the rightness
of being who you are.

Having done this, and feeling one's own
acceptable truth of existing as this particular
set and setting, then exhale, pouring oneself
into the greater condition that—like it or not—
is the form that is the limitless being that
one is always and already."

— Aha

Openness is the Capacity of Oneness

Have you actually thought about it:
what is openness?

Open
up.

Open
to the idea.

Open
to me.

Open
your Heart.

Open
your mind.

I am an open person.
Why are you so closed?
Can't you be a little more open?

These days the word "openness" is easily thrown around in a beautiful, spiritual, flowery, feel-good way, but **what does it *really* mean to be open?** Why does it seem that it is good to be open and bad to be closed? Is it? **How do you know?**

In this and in every moment, you are either opening or you are closing. And, you are either doing it consciously or you are doing it unconsciously. Closing unconsciously is often what creates the suffering in your Life. Opening consciously is what primes you for Ecstasy.

The more open you are to something, the more you feel that you are inherently connected to it. The more you feel that something is part of you, the less you feel separation from it. Your openness is how close you are to a circumstance, to a moment, to an idea or to a person.

There are times when you feel more open with others; you experience more flow in communication, Heart and affinity. The less unconsciously open you are with others the more feelings of separation and isolation exist. The further away you hold yourself, the further away the world pushes you. You become increasingly distant, shut-down, angry and tense. Your opinions become more judgmental, and your positions become more rigid.

The Truth

Openness is the degree of Oneness that is between you and another; it is the measure of how deeply you are in union with Life. **When you do spiritual practice deeply enough, you will inevitably begin to intuit that there is only Oneness, Truth and God.** That is all there is. Any apparent separation is just not even really there. You can know this absolutely as a tacit feeling and as an actual experience. You can know complete Oneness not as a teaching, or as a concept, or as a feeling but as an actuality. It is possible to know perfect, Ecstatic union as *reality*.

Until you know that nothing is separate from you, practice is demanded of you. Practice means to perform feeling Oneness in the midst of experiences where you do not want to be at one. You do it *as best you can*. Practice means to choose to intuit this very teaching: that you are part of all things and all things are part of you. You choose to intuit this especially when you feel it is least so.

An experience of separation happens when you have an unfulfilled desire. So, during those times you are filled with insecurity, need or desire you are in the most optimal condition to practice. Know that you are one with the very condition that is making you feel that you are separate. If you can muster the excruciating effort it can take to carry out this practice, you will transcend your limitations. This means that you will rest throughout all conditions in Oneness, Bliss and Ecstasy.

In Truth, there only is openness. This cannot be explained in any way that would satisfy your intellect. In order to begin to grasp the profundity of this Truth you must practice openness.

Your Nature is Your Nature

To open under any condition
is to live in the Tao.

To live in the Tao is to be in *total relationship*
with the way things actually are.

You are not judging, rationalizing, criticizing, analyzing or assuming any part of Life. You are not leaving out some bits, making up some bits or resisting some bits. You are in complete relationship with all parts of you, your surroundings and others.

The Scorpion & the Dog

Perhaps you know the story of the scorpion and the dog. The story goes like this: there is a scorpion and a dog and they are on one side of a river bank. The scorpion says to the dog, "Mr. Dog, can you give me a ride over to the other side of the river?" The Dog says, "Umm, I am not so sure. You are a scorpion. If I let you climb on my back, you are going to sting me. " The scorpion replies, "Mr. Dog, why would I sting you? I am going across the river with you. If I sting you while we are doing that, not only will you die from my poison, but I will die from drowning because I cannot cross the water like you can." The Dog says, "Of course! Climb on my back." Indeed it is in the scorpion's best interest not to sting the dog, so the dog agrees and wades into the water. The scorpion climbs up the dog's tail and onto his back.

The dog swims half-way through the water, and the scorpion brings up his tail and BOOM! He stings the dog. The dog cries out in shock and in pain: "WHY??! Mr. Scorpion, why did you sting me? Not only am I going to die, but you are going to die too. I am going to die by the water and by the sting. And you are going to die by drowning. Why did you *do* that?" The scorpion answers: "Mr. Dog, don't you get it? I am a scorpion."

The scorpion was acting according to his nature. Many of your problems arise from trying to force your nature to be other than the way it is. You are rarely open to the condition of the way things *actually* are. The perennial teaching of the Tao and of Zen is: open *with* things *the way they actually are*. From such acceptance real change can occur.

(CAUTION) You are used to imposing your own meaning and your own interpretation of what is happening around you onto events rather than simply noticing what is unfolding. This habit limits you to repeatedly live out the story that is in your own head. It is why you continue to get the same unsatisfying results in your Life.

What to Do?

With curiosity and with humility dare to question your own judgments which are so ingrained that you barely know they are there. Allow yourself to simply notice the unfolding conditions of Life. See others as a mystery. Allow yourself to be open to what is possible.

Can you feel the excitement and terror of this? Allow yourself to be quiet and touch the stillness that exists behind the swirling circumstances of your Life.

Now, from this place, let yourself be swept in any direction that would create opening. Be willing to be carried in any direction trusting that your openness, by Grace, will lead to the peace of union.

IT IS not *WRONG* to BE CLOSED

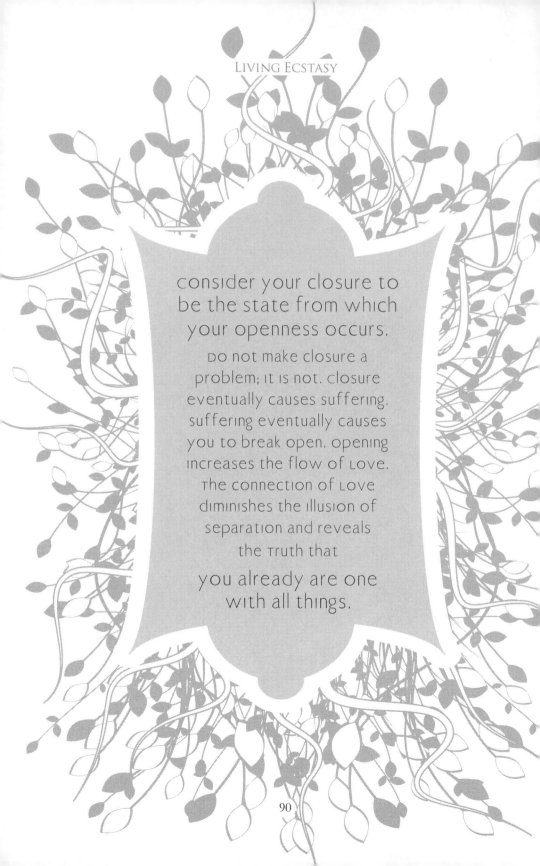

consider your closure to be the state from which your openness occurs.

Do not make closure a problem; it is not. closure eventually causes suffering. suffering eventually causes you to break open. opening increases the flow of love. The connection of love diminishes the illusion of separation and reveals the Truth that

you already are one with all things.

Openness Does not Mean Passiveness

Be aware, openness does not imply that you should ignore the real conditions of your surroundings. Openness simply means to be open and nothing else. If an aggressor is about to attack your family you should not lie placid. You can remain open while choosing whatever action is needed. It is from openness that *divine right action* can be made easily known to you.

If someone is attacking your family, and you close down, your nervous system reacts more slowly. Chemicals triggered by fear are released throughout your body. Your reflexes slow down, your vision becomes myopic, and your awareness is diminished. Closure produces particular responses in all of your systems.

What to Do?

Let Life in; become one with it.

Instead of resisting what is happening, breathe and allow yourself to become one with whatever *is*. Now, again imagine the attack. In the midst of it you are breathing, open and Aware. Your responsiveness is increased; your vision is wider and brighter; and your movements are crisp and accurate. When you are closed it is easy to over-hurt or to under-respond. When you are open you can deliver the right course of action spontaneously from the depth of your consciousness.

Any Condition

Why open under *any* condition? There are certainly a lot of circumstances out there which, by their nature, cause closure, meaning they do not feel good. When your wife is yelling at you; or your parents are disappointed in you; or while your kids are screaming in the car...you do NOT want to open. You want to protect yourself and to move away as quickly as possible. That is natural. You do not want to open to debt, rape or war. Why would you choose to remain open to pain and to horror?

openness is the ultimate act of Love.

Your choice to open under any condition creates the space for conscious Light to enter the moment. Once you begin to practice opening under every condition, you will make a remarkable discovery: nothing is inherently negative or inherently positive. Every single thing just *is*. It is not good or bad, right or wrong. Everything simply is. All aspects of Life are blasts of *isness*, pure isness.

openness is your tool to respond from union rather than from separation.

You will grow to know that it is your responsibility to open under any condition. It is an act of Love, and it is an act of war—war against closure, war against unconscious separation.

Resistance Is Futile

The ancients say, "What you resist persists." Resistance is closure. When you open to things as they are and to others as they are, a wellspring of Wisdom begins to Awaken within you. You are able to speak more clearly. You are able to deal with negative circumstances with much more artistry, fluidity and capacity. You are more connected to the source of Wisdom embodied within you, the learnings you have already received and the evolution you have already sustained.

Openness is the portal for Love; it is the conduit between you and another. Openness is a living tube between you and existence.

when you are open, *everything* is open to you.

While closed, you block the deeper faculties within yourself from being known to you. While open, you have fluid access to: Truth, Wisdom, Knowledge, Grace and Humor. Openness is the funnel for tangible Ecstasy to enter your *daily life*.

Eventually the events of your Life will cause you to open one way or another. Mastery is not an achieved state. If someone tells you that they are a master, run. Mastery is the practice of opening under any condition in this moment. You will never arrive at mastery. You are not meant to. You will always be either unconsciously closing; or you will be opening; or you will be practicing.

To create reality;
to be a master;
to Live your Life
is to choose
moment to moment
to open as Love,
regardless of what
is happening.

96

You Are Accountable

So, Guess What?!

It is your responsibility to recognize when you are *doing* closure. Sometimes you will unconsciously close. It is up to you to recognize that you have stumbled into closure and to open. You are always either giving closure or you are giving Love. You will increasingly notice others' closure. It will be remarkably obvious to you that others are either actively shutting down the portals of Oneness, or they are actively relaxing the illusion of separation. **Again, your responsibility is simply to open.**

You cause the greatest openness by opening yourself.

Why else would you want to open under difficult conditions? In the bed of openness lies peace of mind. Peace is the only genuine fulfillment you have. You will not find real fulfillment in *anything* else. The experience of true Freedom and of deep fulfillment lies in the offering of your openness to all beings regardless of how they show up.

It is especially your responsibility to offer openness when others are: nasty co-workers who steal your ideas; political idiots who are wreaking havoc in the world; unkind bosses who take you for granted; or selfish spouses who ignore your needs...

openness is practical, not metaphysical; it is very practical. Openness brings you fulfillment of the Heart. It brings you Peace by letting you rest in knowing that you cannot change everything nor are you meant to. You *can* change the internal relationship you have with all Beings. Your relationship with others is the ultimate relationship because that is your Universe. Opening to others allows you to be softer and less resistant. You create intimacy when you open as you are in all surroundings as they are. When you are opening, you are doing what you are here to do. Life will flow, and harmony will reign.

HOW YOU BECOME MORE OPEN

practice

The first thing to do is to recognize that openness can be felt in the body mind. It can be felt, and it can be experienced. Think of the eye. The pupil opens and closes in reaction to the light. Similarly your Heart opens and closes according to your reactions and your intentions. When you are unconscious, you open and close with programmed reactions to whatever is around you. When you are conscious you open your Heart by intending to do so. Whichever the case, openness and closure are literally felt in your body-mind.

Imagine that your Lover has just pissed you off. Late to pick you up, your partner forgot your crucial work papers and scratched your new car for the second time. Your natural reaction is anger or to push away. Whatever the case every time others cause you to want to close you have the perfect opportunity to practice opening.

Now imagine that it is your sister who has upset you. You are angry and hurt. Start your practice by seeing her in front of you and begin by breathing her...imagine you are breathing her lungs, and that you are actually in her body. As your lungs expand, hers are expanding. Begin to synchronize your breath and to soften the whole front of your body. While breathing, find the natural rhythm that is between you.

The front of the body is your receptive organ, the receptive channel of the body. Relax. Allow the bridge of the nose to soften and to expand. Allow your jaw to soften and to widen. Allow your throat to relax and to widen. Feel soothed. Allow the front of your chest and sternum to become more spacious, inviting and allowing. Let your solar plexus shine outwardly. Actively invite your sister into the space in and around you. Allow your belly to soften and to fall outward in a motion of warm invitation. Relax your genitals wide open, easing fear. The whole front of your body is soft with inviting attention, ready to receive things as they are. Gently allow yourself to begin to merge with your sister. You cannot change what she did. You need not change how you feel about her. You can choose to open to her.

Remember you may not like it. Openness is not fondness, it is just openness. Allow the front of your body to softly merge with the person or situation with which you have a problem. Then breathe it; feel like you are breathing the space. Breathe in the separation. Breathe out Love. Open through the warmth of your Heart.

 (CAUTION) It is a dangerous misconception that if you open you will lose your ground or condone hateful behavior in others. When you close you do not teach others a lesson. When you close you limit the miracle of Love. Love is connection. When you open you make all solutions possible. You mistakenly think you are in danger if you give up your position, but it is within this very act that your True Freedom is found.

BEYOND CONSTRICTION

Start to feel like your Heart is a warm sun radiating outwards from your whole body in all directions: forward; through the sides; through the back of the spine; upward; and downward. Your whole body is aglow with your Heart radiating outward with warmth and with acceptance in all directions. Allow the radiance of your Heart to warm up the closures in whatever situation is before you. Feel it actually penetrating and softening the relationship between you and another. Let your **intention** be to continue opening rather than to impose any kind of forced change into the situation.

Do not *try* to open. simply open.

Relax as openness itself into the circumstance, and then act from there. When you do this, your actions will be borne from openness. That is how you practically do it. Finally, notice what you say from this place of openness, how you walk from this place of openness, how you make choices from this place of openness and how you naturally treat others from this place of openness.

openness is acceptance, divine acceptance.

Opening under any condition is a gift you give to yourself. You become a conduit of Love. You become a lighthouse of Peace. You become the walking Tao; you bring easy acceptance into the space of closure. You become a channel of the remembrance of how things are. This is all your responsibility. The Sage within you always walks in the Tao. The Warrior within you brings the Tao into moments of closure by opening under any condition. When you walk as open Love, you cannot help but to leave Ecstatic Peace and acceptance in your wake. You, yourself, are waking up to what is prior to the condition of Illumination.

Eventually, you will operate from beyond the current constrictions you now see as your choices. With practice, you will open past the habits and closures that bind you. Until then, you will either unconsciously create closure and suffering in the world, or you will consciously create ease and Ecstasy by your practice of opening under any condition.

Be an open
conduit of Light
and Love for
all beings
throughout
all conditions.

— *five* —

GIVE ANYWAY

"The guests that you have been carrying in your head up to now are your diseases; they are making you sick. They are not allowing you to laugh, they are not allowing you to dance and they are not allowing you to celebrate. What do they allow? Just to be serious and sad–miserable. Look at the point: when you are miserable, there will be self-condemnation.

This is the conspiracy that has been made by the religions against each of you. To be miserable is perfectly okay, to be sad is perfectly okay; your religion has nothing to say about it. But to laugh, to enjoy, or to be drunk with beauty, with bliss, with ecstasy–immediately all your religions start condemning you.

The religions have virtually made the earth a hell. If you were left alone, without any interference from your religions, this very earth could have

been a paradise.... if you are miserable,
condemn it; if you are celebrating,
appreciate it—give a gift to yourself.

when you see somebody celebrating, appreciate
it—just giving him a roseflower would be enough;
give a gift to him. Perhaps this way you will
learn that celebration can be appreciated.
There is no need to condemn it.

your problem is very simple, it is an arbitrary
problem created by others. it is not your problem. it
is not coming out of your natural being.
so today, when there is singing and dancing,
remember, if this self-condemnation comes in,
throw it out. And the way to throw it out is to
jump and jog and enjoy! kill it by your blissfulness.

it is killing your blissfulness. you have every right
to kill it by your blissfulness—by your ecstasy.

– Osho

NOBODY DESERVES WHAT YOU HAVE TO GIVE

People do not deserve everything that you have to give them. Most people do not deserve your gifts. Because people are not deserving, is the very reason why you must give them everything. Forgiveness is not for people who deserve it. That would not be forgiveness. To give means to offer whatever you can even if it is not easy or pleasant to do so. "Give anyway!" is the shout of the Awakened WarriorSage.

Everyone deserves what you have to give. Behind the kinks, habits, patterns, programming and constrictions that form every personality is a dDivine being who deserves all of the Goodness Life has to offer. It is not up to you to judge who is deserving of your attention, your Love and your gifts. Everyone is a part of you, and everyone deserves nothing less than everything you have to give.

What you do not yet grasp is that—like it or not, know it or not—you *have* to give. In fact, you *are* giving. But, are you offering stale, habituated crap or are you offering the gifts of your core essence?

Give anyway! You never need wonder. You never need ask. The Living Truth within you does not care who is on the receiving end. What goes on at that end of the relationship does not bind you into giving or not giving.

The attitudes of the receiver are not even really any of your business.

Your giving is sourced in your own Being. It is not relative to any actions or conditions that are outside of you.

Give to feel the gift of giving. This is not a trick. The real meaning of giving is inherent in the act itself. The actual gift is to give without any attachment to the receiver or to the gift. Give Freely. The magic happens when you offer with a pure Heart. In giving so, you will be gifted.

The trap is that you cannot give so that you may receive. You give for the Ecstasy of giving. Give for giving's sake. Right now make it your secret discipline to give without anyone else knowing about it. Do this and watch your own life explode with miracles. Only remember you cannot give for that reason. There is no reason to give except to GIVE, so *give anyway*.

The Money Question:
Should I give? Should I not give?
Yes! You should give! It is the mandate of your Heart.

The Bottom Line
Give now anyway.

Giving is Sacred and Leads to Ecstasy

Here is an incredible discipline: give of yourself. Do not spend your days waiting to receive. Do not act as the victim who falsely believes that you are not receiving what you need from some outside source. This is a waste of your precious Life force. It is up to you to give. The answer is for you to give. The balm for *your* aching Heart is for you to give your Love, your understanding, your humor, your passion and your patience. Even if you get nothing in return, GIVE ANYWAY. Especially if you get nothing in return, GIVE ANYWAY. Giving is a form of spontaneous return that nurtures the giver; it just happens. Giving is a sacred discipline that causes Ecstasy.

So, Guess What?!

Your fastest route to fully Living Ecstasy is to Love people so deeply and unconditionally that while you are upset at them, and the last thing you want to do is share your vulnerability with them, you give it anyway. It is obviously easy to do when there is harmony, flow, trust and Love. To give anyway is to give when you *really* do not want to, when others are revolting or annoying. That is what matters.

one of the most profound acts of humanity, not divinity, but *humanity* is to give anyway.

It is one of the most profound acts of humility; giving anyway is your sacred offering of humility. There is an active giving that is sourced in your humanity and in your humility. It is also sourced in your humor and in your vulnerability. Giving anyway is your exposed openness. It is your brave choice to dwell naked in your humanity.

what would it be like to give
when someone: cheats on you;
abuses you; steals from you?
what would it be like to give
when that is the last thing
you feel capable of doing?
what would it be like to give
when the other person
doesn't like you?
what would your act of
giving change in the world?

it would change everything.
it would change nothing.

GIVE anyway.

YOU DO HAVE
SOMETHING TO LOSE

Anyone *right* at times? Damn right! when you are right, even if you are *in fact*, right, what you have done is attach yourself to a position. In order to be right you have to have identified yourself with an opinion. When you give anyway you are sure to lose your fixed position. That is what you have to lose: your position. What you fail to realize is that when you lose your position you gain everything! At times you feel so holy and righteous and deserving that you are unwilling to give at all. Do you deserve rightness? Who cares! The better question is: Can you drop your position? Unless you practice loosening and losing your position millions of times, you will never get good at losing yourself.

(CAUTION) As you stubbornly cling to fixed and limited ideas of who you think you are, it is your own Bliss that is sacrificed.

Lose your position. Get good at it. Do not equate losing your position with weakness. Losing your position does not mean losing your centeredness. It does not mean losing your dignity—never do that for anyone. It never ever means sacrificing what is True, never! Losing your position loosens the binding that holds you tightly to the things you do not want. The way to lose your position is to give anyway. Can you feel that?

GIVE WHAT YOU NEVER GOT

Do you want to immediately relieve your depression, your lack or your suffering? Give lavishly whatever it is you feel you are missing in Life. Right now, without excuses or without hesitation, give whatever it is you so desperately wish to receive. You do not need to perfectly understand what to do. A part of you always knows what to do. What matters is that you take a risk. Just take a deep breath and offer something, anything. Find a way.

When you look around and it seems as though everyone else is paired off in a romantic, intimate relationship while you remain sadly alone, begin to focus on giving more depth and care to the relationships you do have. Offer externally whatever your own Heart inwardly desires. When you feel an internal ache that is never soothed because since you were a child you have longed for the approval of your father, find someone who you intuit yearns for the same thing, and give it to them. Give them the validation and the appreciation that you have so long craved. You will know who it is and what to give because whoever you choose will have the same kink as you. Give to others whatever you yearn to receive. Are you angry? What makes you angry? Stop complaining. Choose a way to give in the midst of your self involved irritation. You do not have to change your state or to alter your mood—give anyway.

There is absolutely no valid reason
on earth not to give anyway.
None. Not one. Ever.

People who are GIVING ANyway are too busy
LIVING LIfe to the fullest to collapse under the
weight of their unfulfilled history.

Do you think Mother Teresa had a perfect upbringing with
enlightened parents? Of course not, but that did not stop her, it did
not even slow her down. She just GAVE. She saw raw, unpleasant
need and she filled it without regard to her own preferences or to
her own condition. She did not say, "This is disgusting, and Oh, my
back hurts, I had better stop." She gave anyway.

Sit in the Fire

Stop making up that in order for you to give, some-

thing first has to change. Your mother nags you,

your father hits you, your girlfriend leaves you,

your baby dies, you lose your job, you get

cancer…these are the events that signal you

to immediately begin to offer outward.

Drop your excuses. If this is hard to hear,

open and give anyway.

How It Plays Out
in Your Life

you are overly stressed in Life. what does
Mother Teresa have to do with you?

What to Do?

Give because there is nothing else to do. At the end of the day,
there is nothing else to do. No matter what you have gained, it
will ultimately dissolve. There is nothing you can keep: not one
toy you can accumulate; not one prized possession you can
horde; not even your self-esteem will be yours. Since there is
nothing you are going to be able to hold on to anyway, you
might as well give what is already given. Ultimately, Death
reclaims everything and returns it all to The Great One.
None of it is even yours in the first place. Your health will
deteriorate. Your family will die. When you wake up to the
sobriety that in Death's eyes it is all already given, let it move
you into your humility and into your humanity to do
what will be done: give anyway.

There is a relief in giving anyway. There is a huge relief in setting
aside your self-importance. There is liberation in not having to be run
by being number one. After a while there is a resting and a reckoning
that arises after you give anyway. You become simpler. Giving anyway
always leads to simplicity. If giving makes you more extravagant in
any way, it is a false version of what is said here.

(CAUTION) Whatever brings you to more simplicity is that which
brings you Home.

You Are a Master

You scratch, claw, whine, fight, beg, take, manipulate and struggle to get what you want. You have fully demonstrated that you are masterfully capable of these actions and attitudes when it comes to something you feel you require or deserve. You waste your resources and expend your Life force to get and get and get. You are ruthless in your persistence.

You have everything completely backwards. You are the rat on the wheel chasing nothing. No matter what you get, it will never be enough, and it is pure folly to believe otherwise.

A Secret

To feel full, satisfied, relaxed, replete and peaceful rather than needy, desperate, selfish, driven and worried, you must begin to seek what it is that you can GIVE rather than seeking what you can get. DO whatever it takes to give and give and give. Apply your conniving skills to give, grant, bestow, offer, furnish and provide for others. Eventually you will do this anyway. So catapult yourself from the heavy squander of lack and necessity to the elegance of fullness and opportunity. There is always an opportunity to give. This truly is where you are headed anyway, so why suffer another moment. Enter ECstasy—give now anyway.

Take It from Buddha

Once, a distraught woman went to Buddha. Her grief was the worst kind, her child had died. She begged Buddha to give her child's life back. Buddha said he would grant her wish on one condition. The woman must bring him some beans from a household in which no one had ever died. The woman ran to the first dwelling with hope in her Heart.

An old farmer opened the door. The woman asked, "Pardon me, but has anyone in this household ever died?" The old farmer answered sadly, "Yes, my brother died last spring." The woman felt compassion for him. She understood how he felt. She offered him a kind word and continued on to the next house.

At the next house, a beautiful young woman answered the door. The woman thought that this might be a good sign. She asked, "Pardon me, but has anyone in this household ever died?" The young woman's lovely eyes instantly reddened with tears. She replied, "Yes, my betrothed died in an accident two years ago." The woman was so moved by the beauty's grief that for a moment she forgot her own plight. She took the maiden in her arms to comfort her.

The woman went from home to home, but she could not find a single household that had not been touched by the grief of death. She did not give up. She traveled for years going from place to place until she had covered the land.

When the woman finally returned to Buddha, it was she who spoke. She told him that every household, every family, every person had been visited by death, and that she had no beans. The woman said that even if she could bring her child back, she would not because she knew that eventually her child would die again. She did not want to bear the fresh grief. In comforting others' in their losses, her own pain had begun to heal. The woman spent the rest of her Life helping anyone who had a Loved one die. She Lived a long and fulfilled Life.

Train Yourself to Give

✳ practice

Close your eyes. Expand outward in all directions fully. Hold the whole front surface of your body open. The top of your head is wide open. You are allowing starlight, Truth, God, Goddess, Divinity, Light…to pour down on top of you. You are feeling the thickness of the space above you. It is Divine; you invite it in as if the top of your head is a funnel—a divine funnel, expansive, open and wide. Bring the thickness right down, pouring and filling your body. Light fills your body and pours through your cells. Let it move out into the room. Your Heart is shining brightly.

Feel outward in all directions. Feel that you are a vessel for Ecstasy, a vessel to turn the key to Awakening in everyone around you. It is true, you are. Do not hold anything back. Slowly open your eyes.

Offer acceptance to other beings whether or not they are in the room. Walk around feeling who could use acceptance. Offer it to them in silence. Offer absolute acceptance. Feel what that is like. Keep offering.

That is the way out of the delusion of self-serving and into the Heart of real fulfillment and of real rest, rest of being. When you are always focused on what you are not getting, you are at unrest. There is a demand of attention and a scampering of neediness.

In the moment you give anyway, you are released of the burden of the very thing you wish to get. It is an Ecstatic moment.

You are *Living* Ecstasy.

— *six* —

WINK

"why are the passes of the old shamans called magical passes, don juan?" I asked him on one occasion.

"they are not just called magical passes," he said, "they are magical! they produce an effect that cannot be accounted for by means of ordinary explanations. these movements are not physical or mere postures of the body; they are real attempts at reaching an optimum state of being."

"the magic of the movements," he went on, "is a subtle change that the practitioners experience on executing them. it is an ephemeral quality that the movement brings to their physical and mental states, a kind of shine, a light in their eyes. this subtle change is a touch of the spirit. it is as if the practitioners, through the movements, reestablish an unused link with the life force that sustains them."

He further explained that another reason that the movements are called magical passes is that by means of practicing them, shamans are transported, in terms of perception, to other states of being in which they can sense the world in an indescribable manner.

"Because of this quality, because of this magic,"
don juan said to me, "the passes must not be
practiced as exercises, but as a way
of beckoning power."

"But can they be taken as physical
movements, although they have never
been taken as such?" I asked.

"You can practice them any way you wish,"
don juan replied. "The magical passes enhance
awareness, regardless of how you take them.
The intelligent thing would be to take them as
what they are: magical passes that on being
practiced lead to the practitioner to
drop the mask of socialization."

"what is the mask of socialization?" I asked.

"The veneer that all of us defend and die for," he said.
"The veneer we acquire in the world. The one that
prevents us from reaching all our potential..."

– carlos castaneda

A Portal to Ecstasy

Wink with the wink of your soul, and you may find that the whole world is already winking back at you.

The Wink is happening all around you. If you really peer at anything you see, and you drop your thinking mind—you just let your judgments relax and fall back into the place from where the thinking mind is arising—you will begin to recognize and to deeply feel that the very core of existence is winking at you. The Great Mystery is letting you know that *It* is benign; *It* is benevolent; *It* is shining the smile deep within your Heart.

A Secret

wink—
not just
with your eye
wink with
your whole
being.

Reach down into your depths and pull out: a wink. To wink is to know that regardless of what is going on in life, that within you resides the sacred empire of the soul. There is a secret mystery that underlies all things, all beings, all times and all places. Underneath your worst dilemma, there is a behind-the-scenes secret which is begging to be noticed. It is the secret of divinity and the secret of perennial knowledge. It is the secret of the ever-giggling fool in the play of the court of the Divine. To wink is to know that the deepest love wants for itself to be known to you. The wink penetrates your suffering even while you hide away in your closet of self-reflection.

THE INHERENT CELEBRATION WITHIN EACH MOMENT

The wink is a moment that can happen between two friends in the middle of a terrible fight when they realize that their Love is deeper than the tension and the strife that is between them, and that their conflict will pass. The solid ground of Being, from which their relationship was formed and arose, is the wink. The wink is the delightful tickle that lets you know that it is okay to be okay, and it is okay that everything everywhere is as it is. The wink reveals that absolutely everything is *beyond okay.*

There is an inherent celebration in the wink.

The wink is the realization that you are not your preferences and you are not your behaviors.

In the midst of an angry argument the wink can be the clink of two finely made crystal champagne glasses being gently met as each friend silently Awakens to the something that is greater than the moment in which they are caught. It is the little recognition that says, "Aaaahhhh, this too is a secret champagne moment." The wink reveals that this is a highly refined moment of recognition of what really and truly matters in the midst of anything.

The wink is the reverent knowledge that even the most cherished things you possess will all pass from being. Your health, Lovers, wealth, career, family and self-esteem will all disappear. Each external attribute gained in life will eventually dissolve. Every internal attribute achieved *will all dissolve.* Every earned and cultivated possession will melt away as surely as it appeared.

What is left when that happens? What remains is the Wink, the Wink of Divinity. It is the Wink that pierces through the illusion of everything temporary. In every moment you are receiving the Wink. If you are carefree enough, haphazard enough, silently awake enough, you will wink back. You will wink back to the Wink that is winking back at you. It is in the moments that you allow the Wink to penetrate, and you break your habit of self-importance in order to wink back, that both winks dissolve into THE WINK that is all EXISTENCE.

THE ETERNAL WINK
PENETRATES ALL

The Wink is humor,
the humor of Divinity.
To wink is to know
the humor of all things
personal and impersonal.
The Wink is a gentle jolly
stride through life, Free of
the heaviness of burden or
notions of obligation.

What to Do?

Wink. Wink whenever you are in the midst of an amazing situation. At the height of your pleasure look around and wink. Reveal the part of you that is Eternal.

Through the wink share the only part of you that is REAL.

Say to the world: "Yes, I am here, *and* I {**wink**} know who I am. I am not 'happy' or 'found' any more than I am 'sad' or 'lost.' I {**wink**} am." When you wink for no other reason than *you* are, you will realize that whether or not anyone winks back at you—they actually are winking. Everything and everyone everywhere is always winking. Some part of their Being or some part of existence is always playfully reminding you of who you really are by saying: "Hey, here's a **wink**!"

Wink at the highest moment when everything is fantastic. Pour your silent brilliance into your wink and casually send it across the room. Even without moving an eyelid, you can instantly lift the load of another by giving the wink of you Heart. Share the silent knowledge that everything is going to be alright, that everything is actually extraordinary.

Winking is the very profound work of saints because winking does not require any prerequisite, such as a positive state of being. Winking simply requires the relaxation into that which formed you, that which is forming this very moment.

The Mystery that is bubbling through is the **Wink,** the champagne of existence.

Make sure to wink when things are difficult or unpleasant. such conditions actually provide the most pristine and wondrous opportunity to wink. when you feel down, trashed, exhausted, needy or betrayed—wink. when you are full of tension, full of fear or full of confusion recognize it as the opportune moment to impact the world and wink.

When you are in the middle of an argument with a Lover or a friend and you are caught in the abyss of your position versus their position, **wink**. When you are caught in the tension of the separation between what you want and you are not getting, and what they want and what they are not getting, **wink**. **Wink** from the place in you that is already free from dilemma. **Wink** from the place in you that is already Love. There is a place within you that is not trying to get Love and that is not trying to get to Freedom. This undeniable part of you is, at all times, Freedom and Love incarnate. From that place, **wink** to the one you are fighting. They may not receive it in the way you want them to, but some part of them is going to receive that **wink** and it will begin to melt their barriers and to soften their resolve. Realize that even if they lash out, it has nothing to do with the **wink**.

The Wink: A Love Story

Listen to a True story about Love

There are Love stories happening all around you. Some of the stories are a little longer, and some are a little shorter. Some have different twists and turns, but in the end there is only one story of Love. It is the story of *Consciousness Loving Light*, and of *Light Loving Consciousness*. It is Awareness infusing Light, and it is Light radiating Awareness. It is Love and Freedom showing up as different forms in play.

The story itself might go like this: She lives with a demanding goof; one day he likes a certain food and the next day he does not. No matter who he is, he has hundreds of habits and preferences that are just like that. Can you imagine the cultivation of surrender and depth she has to have to even tolerate him? Can you imagine Living with that? And what about her?! She is as unpredictable, as unforgiving and as relentlessly intense as the weather. How does he bear-up day after day?

The Heart of this or of any Love story is the Wink. Whether he or she knows it, they are the wink winking at each other through all conditions. Ecstasy is realized as one or both become more Aware of the wink that they are. This is every Love story including yours.

143

AT THE CENTER OF IT ALL

Do you want to know the straight, quick path to never-ending joy? Find the wink in the midst of Life. Forget all of your growth techniques. (CAUTION) You do what you learn while you are still at your work-shops or at church, and then you go home and tear each other apart. What you need to do is to drop your position in the middle of the worst moment. When you wink you say to your Loved one: "Life is fleeting. I Love you through my crunchiness. I Love you more than I want to be right about my position. I am ready to Live from the Heart."

Sit in the Fire

As a Spiritual Warrior, in the name of Love, do what you need to do to bring Freedom and Light even if it is not what you want to do. That is the moment when you take a sip from the Well of Unreasonable Happiness. That is the moment of liberation from all that binds you. When you wink, you let go of your position and you enter Ecstasy.

Wake Up to the Wink

The wink is the recognition of *your* Eternal Oneness. The wink says, "Yeah, I am dying, and you are dying." What remains when everything dissolves? *That* is what you are winking about. It is *not* just some trivial wink. In that wink you are transmitting: "Wake up! There is a bigger secret. God is going on right now." Continue releasing your position in that wink with Humor and with Love. Wink to say, "Yeah, we are dying. Let's Love." You do not even have to stop what you are doing. Without stopping, once in a while, wink. Be real. Wink spontaneously. Transmit Freedom in your wink.

> You are winking to give an injection of *the real* into the midst of a stuck position whether it is yours or it is theirs. The position may not even be wrong, it is simply stuck. You are being the one to give the breath of fresh air where it has grown stale. You may even have a *valid point*. The validity of your opinion will never change the world. By staying positioned around your view, you collapse your point with the weight of your fixation. By becoming heavy around your fixation you collapse it from the Freedom of on-going you-ness. The more anchored you are in your position, the less space you have for evolution. If you are to evolve, you must loosen your fixations. This is what it means to undermine everything high and low. You undermine your own philosophy.

This is what it means to Live Ecstasy and to let Ecstasy Live you. In the moment, you drop your position. What you will feel is a little micro moment of Freedom. Do that in the midst of your workday. Literally, wink at yourself. Look in the reflection in the computer screen and wink. See your own likeness and wink. It seems simple. It is a doorway to Infinity.

The wink is the only constant that ever was. It is the only constant that ever will be. It is the only constant that will remain when all things pass. The wink is the ever-bubbly shine of the Mystery. It is the ever-effervescent tickle that courses through your veins.

The Wink is
the pulse of Life,
the Wink is
the substance of
matter, of all
organic
creation.
The Wink is
the emptiness of
the sea in which
we abide.

Here's
winking
at you.

— *seven* —

ANY MOMENT NOW

"under, and back of, the universe of time,
space and change, is ever to be found the
substantial reality—the fundamental truth."

"substantial" means: actually existing.
"Reality" means: the state of being real;
true, enduring; valid; actual.

He (man) sees that nothing really is,
but everything is becoming and changing.
Nothing stands still—everything is being born,
growing, dying—the very instant a thing
reaches its height, it begins to decline...
nothing is permanent but change.

He sees all things evolving from other
things, and resolving into other things—
a constant action and reaction; inflow
and outflow; building up and tearing down;
creation and destruction; birth, growth
and death. Nothing endures but change.
And if he be a thinking man, he realizes
that all of these changing things must
be but outward appearances or
manifestations of some underlying
power—some substantial reality.

—The Kybalion

The Hymn of Your Soul

Any moment now... Any moment now... Any moment now, is your soul's hymn. Any moment now is the pregnant expectation of the miracle that is arising. It feels exciting and perhaps a little uneasy. Any moment now... It is the opportunity for...anything you can imagine. It is the temptation of Ecstasy calling you all the way Home. It is the constant rare occasion for you to be absolutely altruistic, absolutely divine and absolutely humane.

Any moment now is full, positive expectation. It instantly draws to you the providence and the panache of now. *Any moment now* is your call on Providence to deliver. Your own surrender is what is birthing this moment. *Any moment now* is your declaration of fullness and of richness. *Any moment now* is your expectation that something miraculous is going to happen now and now and now, or at least *any moment now*.

Your positive expectation of a miracle, *any moment now,* impregnates all moments that go forth from now in all directions, into the future and into the past. Your eager anticipation penetrates out into the future with the expectation of greatness; with the expectation of generosity; with the expectation of prosperity; and with the expectation of fulfillment. It does not carry any lingering shadow of fear. Your earnest anticipation of *any moment now* reaches into the past softening the impact of the blows and healing the sting of the wounds.

Any moment now is looking out with the eyes of your Heart into the Mystery, knowing that the Mystery itself is benevolent. The Great Mystery is benevolent to your movement, to your cause and to your very existence. In this benevolence you are perfectly held. You are aligned with the Great Mystery Itself. You were born into it from it. You are a product of Goodness. Let your soul sing its song: any moment now.

The Ears of Your Heart

Any
moment
now

is a commitment to listen
and to hear.

It is listening to another's
true voice.

It is listening to the ever
present silence.

It is hearing the whisper

of pain

and the scream of
pleasure.

It is feeling the roar of
Love wanting to
flood you.

It is hearing the rush of
space filling you.

It is hearing Death
soothe you.

It is listening to time
taunt you.

Any
moment
now

is your merry acceptance
of Life's invitation.

Any moment now is you declaring: "I'm ready to receive it ALL!" Any moment now is you saying, "Whatever has happened is finished. Whatever is coming has yet to arrive. This is a fresh moment. I am ready. I am ready to listen. I am ready to move, unbound, in any direction. I am ready to open under any condition. I am ready right now to fill the room with who I am. I am ready to serve. I am now willing to abide in Love and to let Love abide."

WHY YOU DON'T GET
WHAT YOU WANT

Are you ready to hear why you do not get what you want? With all of your hard work, scheming, effort, improvement, training and positivity, why don't you get what you want? Or, for you New Agers, since you create your own reality, why don't you manifest what you're focusing on?

Take this quiz

Choose one of the following:

☐ Any moment now.
☐ Any moment now, I will realize
   that it has all begun.
☐ Any moment now, it all begins.

Here it is. You do not get what you want because when you decide on, wish for or ask for what you want, you are doing it from a kinked and limited fraction of yourself that is so constricted down into what you consider to be reality that you are blinded to Who You really Are.

Essentially, it is a limitation (your idea of you)
asking the illusion (what you believe is real)
to fill an imagined lack.

What to Do?

When you rise up and cry out, "Any moment now!"

you can crack open and sink down into the depth of

Who You Are. You are Infinite. At this point, you may find

that you no longer really have any requests.

When you do, and you are coming from the fullness

and prosperity that you are, your command will already

be fulfilled. You will simply enjoy Life as you expectantly

await the unfolding fruition of your **intention**,

all the while humming: *any moment now*.

Look again at the quiz. If you chose the third option: "Any moment now, it all begins," you, yourself, are waiting to begin to really Live. You are waiting for some condition or conditions to be met, so that you can then be happy and give your gifts. You sometimes play the victim or the fool acting burdened or confused. You are miserable a good portion of the time. Whatever fleeting happiness you do experience is shallow and dependent upon the conditions and people around you.

When you choose the second option, "Any moment now, I will realize that it has all begun," it is clear that you have investigated a bit into what Life is about. However, you quickly and lazily settled for the answers you found. Secretly or overtly you feel yourself to be quite conscious and, in some way, ahead of others. You are still more focused on the micro view of your tiny wants, needs and personality rather than lifting your true eyes to behold the vision of what is really going on.

If you tried to pick all of the answers, you do demonstrate a bit of daring flare. Perhaps you are willing to probe beneath the surface value of the programmed mind set. Yet, no doubt you are aware of this and quite proud of yourself for doing so. You can be trapped here by arrogance and the delusion of depth. You often lack humility and simplicity.

Sit in the Fire

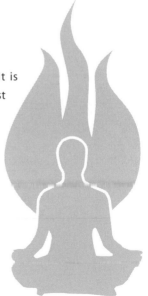

"Any moment now" is YOU, as yourself announcing: It is done. Whatever you chose, you are not *wrong*. You must naturally and sincerely experience the restrictions of the karmic cage you currently inhabit, so that you can choose to push past. You must burn the weighty layers of you psychic entrapment. Stay in the fire. Awareness is your torch.

"Any moment now" is YOU, as yourself announcing: It is done.

THERE IS ONLY ONE MOMENT

There is only this moment. There is only one moment. When you experience something different, you are experiencing a different aspect of this one moment. There only is, has ever been or ever will be this one moment. Choose to feel that. Relax, breathe and allow your mind to still. Inhale. Your inhale literally is incarnation. Every incarnation happens in this moment. Exhale, and let it all go. Die completely with the full release of your breath. Breathe in, be born and Live. Breathe out, let go and die. Do it again and again. This is reincarnation.

Now, feel the moments in between your breaths. Those are the only ones that are really going on. Any moment now! It is a profound koan. It is more than a paradox. It is more than an unanswerable question which has an answer that leads to Truth.

Any moment now.
something is going to happen,
but as soon as you recognize that,

poof!

it is already gone.

No! It is already gone. If you are in a perpetual state of any moment now, not only are you in the now, you are *alive* in the now.

A Secret

Any moment now is the activation of magic. Any moment now is the recognition that all of the moments that have ever occurred in your life have been formulated and conspiring to make you happy, now. Any moment now is you tricking you into your own heart with a wink. The inertia of all occurrence has been conspiring, working its delicious web of intrigue, so that any moment now the accumulation of all past experience is going to burst through your open heart into this present instant as unreasonable happiness. Greetings, welcome to the magical kingdom of now.

Live Each Moment as if
It Is Your First and Last

Come face to face with the reckoning of your mortality. Face death. Many spiritual schools and teachings are full of promises of an afterlife: some form of heaven; some form of nirvana; or some form of future ascension into another domain or reality. That may all be true; however, to dwell upon any of that is not the way. It is a sticky trap for your mind and your ego. Certainly, it could all be true. It could also simply be a fantasy of the mind of consciousness, a more fanciful way to protect the on-going ego after death.

Death can reveal to you
the sacredness of the moment and
the preciousness of being human.

You will know the preciousness of having bills, rage, disappointment, stress and a fat ass. You will know the reward of Life with all of your foibles included. You will know the value of Life as it is, even with all of the things that you don't have that you think you need.

You will know the wisdom of
the real value of all things when you
keep Death close by chanting,

Any
moment
now.

Death is Welcome Here

Feel Death, immanent mortal death. Feel you Living and Dying as a human being. Feel the urgency of each moment that, really, without a doubt, all things are arising and falling. Look at a tree. It will live, it will grow, it will bloom, and it will die. It arises and it falls. All of creation, including this moment, is doing the same. The arising is the event of the moment. Where is your attention?

We tend to shy away from Death. Very few people have even seen or touched a dead human body let alone a dead animal. Most edible meat comes pre-packaged—all wrapped and prepared. Very few see the slaughter process at all. Because you have removed yourself from Death, you have removed yourself from the icy cold inspiration that is Death. Death is an icy cold inspiration. Death should shake you. It should rattle you. Death should bring you to the cold tremor of immanent mortality.

What if the end of this day is really all there is...really...all there is and nothing else? Wake up! Wake up from the slumber of your mediocrity and from the slumber of your fuzziness.

 (CAUTION) You can allow yourself to have terrible events and circumstances to Awaken you, or you can come to Death yourself. YOU knock on Death's door.

Come to death yourself. Every morning when you wake up, really WAKE UP. Knock loudly on the door of Death. Invite Death when things start getting a little too stressful or when things start getting a little too serious. Invite Death when what you are experiencing is self-complaints over small matters such as arguments with family members or conflicts around money.

Knocking on Death's door can open the hidden doorway to genuine gratitude. The use of Death is your responsibility. If you use Death wisely, you may experience profound gratitude throughout all of the conditions and experiences of life. Death is an ever-present teacher. It is up to you to make valuable use of all teachers. Do so by opening your Heart in invitation to the opportunity of Death. Give freshness to the moment when you know it has gone stale. Be willing to release your hold on all your sacred cows, and then the teachings of Death may Grace you. That sense of self-importance that you naturally carry around will shrink. You will feel deep gratitude and the immense holiness of the one and only moment.

What to Do?

If you knock on Death's door, you will be granted a
sobering gift. You will know that THIS is going to pass.
Death provides levity. The presence of Death allows you to
realize that the meager events of your Life are meaningless.
These events and conditions have already passed from
existence in Death's eyes. So what to do?
Rather than resist Death, you be the one
to encourage Death to enter.
Live each moment feeling Death.

YOUR EDGE

In the witness of the breadth and scope of your entire Life, are any matters actually meaningful? You can transcend your own self-importance. Your self-importance is a habit. When you did not get what you wanted as a baby, you cried, fussed or threw tantrums. Once you became an adult, you continued this. You just became more sophisticated with your tantrums. You became more complicated with your complaints. You give more metaphysical or real meaning to your dramas. You become a sophisticated adult baby carrying around this self-importance while focusing on of all the things that you are not getting or on all the things that are not going your way. If you look at the scope of life, these things are really just not important.

Self-importance is when you attach yourself to these minor things that keep you locked-down into the mundaneness of Life.

The Money Question

Without your self-importance and the dramas surrounding it, what would be the purpose of your Life?

There is a practical value to this. If you are in the middle of a tension-filled fight with your Lover and you choose to wake up beyond the narcissism of whatever you are not getting that you want, and you look at your partner and see them as deteriorating—in any moment your Lover could just drop dead—then BOOM! All of a sudden you do wake up. You incarnate; you Live as if this is the only moment. Doing this erases your own personal history. The moment you embody and you Live as if this instant is the only moment; everyone's personal history is

---

The Bottom Line

Drop the self-indulgent habit of your own self-importance.

continued...

erased. Exist in a fresh space to see everyone as they are without the baggage of the momentum that you are carrying about them. You judge and label the momentum of their arising according to your own beliefs and experiences; however, in Truth they are not responsible for whatever you are carrying about them.

In order to make a choice that will carry you beyond your self-importance you will be at your edge.

Beyond your edge is where all real growth occurs.

Beyond your edge is where all change happens. As long as you are comfortable, which means that you are simply re-enacting an ego-driven pattern, no matter what you think you are doing, you are not engaged in Bliss.

You will know when you are at your edge because you will feel nervous, uncomfortable, angry, righteous, scared or belligerent. This is good. Do not sink down into the weight of the feelings. Instead, see these feelings as your signal to leap. You will not want to—never mind that. And never mind whatever is going on around you. Choose to offer more than you think you can give, and you will widen to the Peace, Prosperity and Ecstasy that is your birthright. You can always find your edge at any moment now.

Awakening Is a Choice

To Live Ecstasy is to drop your habit of self-absorbed self-importance by acknowledging the meaning that is inherent within the core of you, that you are cut from the Heart to Live as the Heart. To be Living Ecstasy is to make art out of your kinks instead of believing that your kinks are the limitations of your Life or the authentic attributes of your character. Fill the room with who you are. Without hesitation, open under the condition of right now, and fill the whole room and beyond. Offer you through your open Heart for the sake of all Beings. It is the only thing that matters, and it will bring you profound tranquility and unspeakable joy. Give anyway. Things will come up. Give anyway. Wink and laugh, the deep laugh of your essence. How good would that feel? You are Ecstasy. Anything else you are experiencing is something that you are actively doing over the top of it. And that is why, any moment now…

Notice (ANY MOMENT NOW) that (ANY MOMENT NOW) throughout your quest to reveal your True Ecstatic nature, there is a single (ANY MOMENT NOW) common denominator: your choice. You (ANY MOMENT NOW) must choose (ANY MOMENT NOW) to do what it takes (ANY MOMENT NOW) to be the one (ANY MOMENT NOW) who simply is authentically you. Eventually (ANY MOMENT NOW) your practice will undo itself, and the Light of your Ecstatic Heart will shine (ANY MOMENT NOW) for all Beings. Know this, now that you have read this: you can never again pretend that you don't know. You do know. Awakening (ANY MOMENT NOW) is your choice. You are the Light of the world. From now it will be preposterous if (ANY MOMENT NOW) you try to hide your Light.

— eight —

EMBODY ECSTASY

"Nothing real can be threatened. Nothing
unreal exists. Herein lies the peace of God.

Miracles are natural. When they do not occur
something has gone wrong.

Miracles are thoughts. Thoughts can
represent the lower or bodily level of
experience, or the higher or spiritual level
of experience. One makes the physical,
and the other creates the spiritual.

Miracles transcend the body. They are sudden
shifts into invisibility, away from the bodily
level. That is why they heal.

There is no substitute for truth.

If you cannot hear the voice of God it is
because you choose not to listen."

—A Course in Miracles

What is Your Body?

You are obsessively over-identified with believing that your body is you. You believe that somehow you are contained inside this thing, your body. Living Ecstasy is your body; your body is a conduit of the very essence of what all of Existence is.

Ecstasy is actually the large hologram showing up in a small version as your, so-called, limited and finite, body. Living Ecstasy quite literally is the container and the condition that you already walk around in. Of course, you may not be feeling this at all times. Once you start to plunge into the wisdom that lies at the core of your breath—the unexplainable energy that lies at the Heart of every cell, you will undoubtedly find the answer. Plunge deeper and smaller with your consciousness into the absolute mystery, magic, energy and incredible, incredible emptiness that lies in the Heart of every atom, and you will start to discover that Ecstasy starts from the inside out. The inside you have is the body. The outside is the world. The inside is you. The outside is what shows up in your world. It is also...you.

Living Ecstasy is not a concept or a goal. It is not a state or an emotion. It is not something you find or something that is exterior to you. Living Ecstasy is what you are made of.

Living Ecstasy starts
as the space and content
within every cell of your body.

You cannot grasp this—you do not need to,
you already know it.

The Bottom Line
Recognize that Living Ecstasy can only happen when your body is involved.

THE SECRET TEACHING
OF BREATH

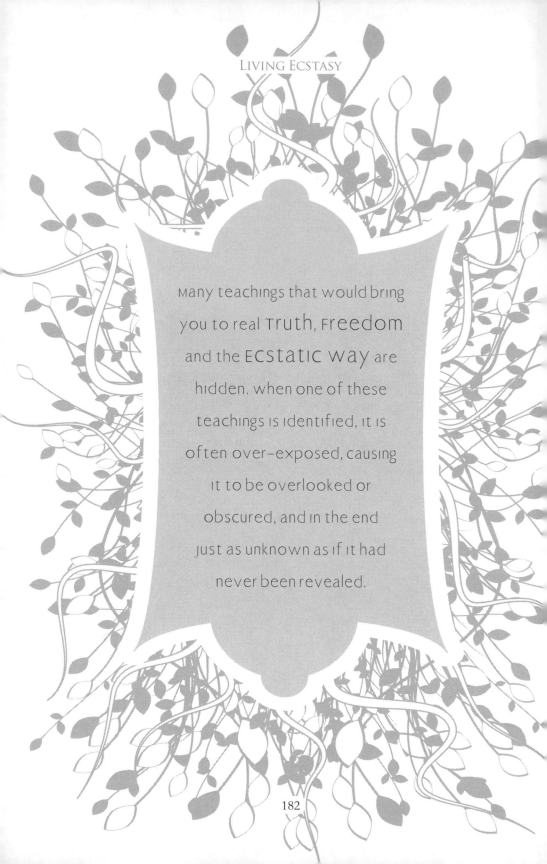

Many teachings that would bring you to real Truth, Freedom and the Ecstatic Way are hidden. when one of these teachings is identified, it is often over-exposed, causing it to be overlooked or obscured, and in the end just as unknown as if it had never been revealed.

There is powerful wisdom within your body; true yoga and conscious breathing are such teachings. You have probably exercised. You might go to yoga class, or you might have even tried to do a breathing exercise or two, but unless you are walking around in absolute Blissed-out pleasure that permeates every other condition of your Life every minute of every day, then you have not yet properly exploited the profound learnings to be gained from breathing.

Yoga means union.
Yoga is the practice of rediscovering
the knowledge of oneness that is locked
in your body. It is the Awareness of
the natural harmony of all things
in relationship to you. Yoga is whatever
practice brings you into a greater
consciousness of the way
things already are.

The most simplistic path of directly entering the arising moment as it is unfolding is through your breath. The way to most quickly relax into the pre-existing condition of Living Ecstasy is through your breath. Conscious breathing is the yoga of energy in the body. Often, the energies in your body are either flowing in reverse, or they are clogged. When your energies are flowing in reverse it means that you are more apt to be unconsciously caught in the contrived world. Your thoughts and actions are not your own. You are the puppet of programming, conditioning and sentimentality. When your energies are slowed or clogged it creates some level of dis-ease within one or more of your bodies—physical, emotional or spiritual.

When your energies are freely flowing you are clear, Awake and powerful. You are Free to move in any direction. You are neither binding another nor bound yourself. You create more peace, understanding and FUN in the world. You cause less pain, damage and suffering.

continued...

You can increase the natural Free flow of the energies in your body by doing a simple breath practice. Relax the front of your body. Relax the muscles of your face. Allow your belly to soften and your chest to open. Breathe in down the front of your body. Allow the breath to travel down until it reaches your genitals. Feel the ecstatic quality of your own breath. Relax your hips. As you exhale, your breath travels up the back of your spine and out the top of your head. Allow your breath to leave your body by spouting like a beautiful fountain out the top of your head. Don't worry about getting it just right. It is simple, yet the practice alone will bring up your resistance. Stay with it. If you get frustrated, continue to breathe while you wink and hum, "Any moment now…" If you botch the practice for a moment, you'll at least have a laugh at yourself.

A full breath is basic yoga. As a first step, it won't necessarily get you Enlightened. At this stage it has more to do with energy circulation, a vital beginning. This yogic breathing improves the capacity of Free flowing energy to increase the accessibility of your Life force and to Free up your bound attention.

Conscious breath practice is so powerful that it is impossible to convince you of its profundity. Chances are that through arrogance, ignorance or laziness you will pooh pooh this important practice and miss altogether one of the greatest secrets that will ever be revealed to you. However, if you continue to practice, all knowledge and complete joy is yours. When you are not Living as the shining embodiment of the Ecstasy the Lives you, you are not fully Living the Life that was meant to be yours. Breathe.

The Only Bondage that Matters

You are bound by knots of attention. Whenever you identify with anything or anyone in any way, your fixed attention binds you to it. When this association becomes a habit, the energetic pattern that is formed binds you even tighter. Your units of attention become caught and unavailable for you to use elsewhere. Breath practice will naturally and automatically loosen and release these bound knots of attention. When you begin to do breath practice, you will begin to feel bodily Ecstasy. You will begin to experience emotional Ecstasy. As you mature and stabilize in your practice you will begin to Live your entire Life more and more in a rested state of unconditional Ecstasy that will permeate everything around you.

There are certain yogic systems—Taoist yoga, Chinese yoga, Indian yoga—that break all of this down into minute detail. Many of you have an affinity for complexity, and that is wonderful. Do whichever one you are drawn to, whichever one you find to be FUN. Keep in mind that eventually you will find your edge in whatever practice you choose. All of your gain will be made when you practice past that threshold. It all depends on the attitude of your own Heart. If you are ready and committed, then what you are shown here is more than enough to take you to embodied Enlightenment and the responsibilities that lay beyond.

What to Do?

What you will have to face, in order to realize that boundless Bliss is a way of Life, are various obstacles and thresholds. An obstacle is anything that would distract you from practicing. Whatever stops you from filling the room with Who You Are or from giving anyway is your obstacle. Then, there is a threshold to surpass. A threshold is anything which is between you and the conscious experience of bodily Ecstasy. Eventually your practice will get to the point where, instead of stops and starts that take a while, in a few seconds you can recalibrate your breath, re-establishing the natural circuitry that allows your Life force to flow through you. This, in turn, will allow everything inside and around you to Awaken. You and everything around you will be nourished on many levels.

THE SECRET BEHIND THE SECRET

The secret that is rarely taught is that, no matter what practice, teaching or religion you choose, the key is feeling outward from the Heart. This is the Enlightenment, the Oneness. Feel your Heart to be bright and warm. Feel your Heart smiling and shining its radiance in all directions. When the body dies, this remains. This is superior to any other primary practice, belief, teaching or system. This is the primary practice of importance—the Heart.

A Secret

The Heart is not an organ alone. Your own Heart is the Heart of existence. It is also known as Love and Freedom. Your Heart is existence, the way it is, feeling outward from you. Your Heart is shining and feeling all beings in all places in all conditions.

When you start to do such Heart practice, the most important practice, you will grow through predictable and unknown barriers and thresholds. At first you will encounter attention that is particularly encased around the self. This is the most constricted and shrunken span of your attention. You will have to open past obsessive selfish thoughts and behaviors that center on you and on your relationships. The more deeply you practice the more quickly you will face increasing circles of Awareness that will direct you to focus on the care and concern of others. Without the conscious shine of the Heart, both care and concern are themselves just a trap for your widening attention.

continued...

CAUTION Whether your attention is caught on yourself or on another, what happens is that you follow your thoughts. "I'm too fat. I don't feel good. He looks sad. She is beautiful." That is the binding of attention. In that moment you create subject and object, and you enter the world of duality. You are now trapped in the mock, illusionary world of finite potentials where everyone has forgotten their true nature.

What to Do?

Even the explanation of a condition such as duality
is heavy and confusing. The mind reels and the body sags.
What to do. Shine your Heart. The penetrating beauty of you
shatters all illusion and is all you will ever need.

Drop the Ascension Trip

It is wasteful and immature to spend your Life obsessively trying to attain some mystical higher state or to ascend to some higher plain.

your Life is sacred.

It is the gift you have to give. For practical reasons alone, begin with what you *know* to be so. You are here. You have a body. When life doesn't work, you and those around you experience suffering. Everything here, in this reality that you are in, is experienced through the body and through relationship. All of your emotions are felt in the body or are stored in the body. You experience *everything* in relationship to something or to someone else. Experience does not exist here without relationship. You are here now. You might or might not go somewhere else later, but you surely are here now.

Believe whatever you like about where you might end up after Death or after any change of state, but do not exhaust your precious resources pinning after it. When you wait to have your joy later, by investing completely in sentiments such as, "In heaven things will be better...I am a being of Light that does not really belong here..." you separate yourself from Ecstasy. You live for a fantasy of what might be or of what might come. Even if you are correct, you waste the precious gift of Life that is happening here and now.

What to Do?

Drop your future trips.

Pour everything you've got into this moment.

Fill the room with who you are, and

whenever something arises that would

stop you from that, give anyway.

Sure you've got to plan for the future.

Just don't *live* there.

The truth is you can't Live there,

so stop spinning your wheels. Life is happening

here and now through your body and

through your relationships.

WHATEVER IS REAL IS EMBODIED

We are all different strings on the lute of the Divine.

Your spirituality must come through your body. The value of being human is that you can feel, express, give, receive and experience.

Forget the metaphysics of *why* you should do things. Start simply with what you empirically know to be true from the results you can tangibly see. Things don't always start in consciousness; some things start in action. So, let's reverse engineer this.

For example, if you are having a hard time with money, instead of taking a metaphysical approach, endeavor to practically solve the problem in reality. Get a job; pay off your debt; stop overspending; or cut up your credit cards. It might not seem so glamorous, yet often these fundamental steps are actually the most spiritual solutions you can offer. Some part of you always knows what to do.

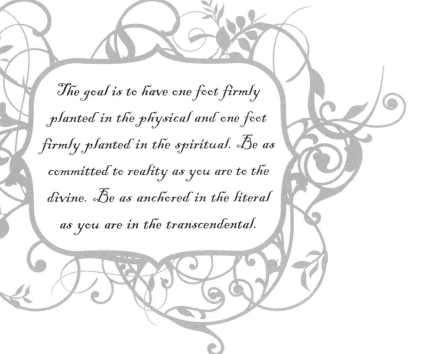

The goal is to have one foot firmly planted in the physical and one foot firmly planted in the spiritual. Be as committed to reality as you are to the divine. Be as anchored in the literal as you are in the transcendental.

Living Ecstasy is the natural state of harmony in the body. When you allow yourself to meditate this Living Ecstasy from within every cell outward, for the sake of all beings, you become more casually inspired to act from what is already good for the body.

The Money Question
What is naturally good for the body?
❏ You will start to know that you already intuitively do know.
❏ You know what to pick up to eat, and what to leave behind.
❏ You know when you need to rest.
❏ You know when you need to move.
❏ You know when you need to work.
❏ You know when you need to play.

You will see more and more clearly what it is that brings you closer to the part of you that is always Unreasonably Happy. When your body is open, the conditions that cause and promote Living Ecstasy automatically arise in you. Your body is the Living conduit of Living Ecstasy. Your body is made from Living Ecstasy. Your body is what gives anything and everything reality. When you are more open, it feels better, and you feel better for no apparent reason other than the natural spontaneous openness which is happening. This is Living Ecstasy living You.

When you begin to acknowledge that reality is embodied, the Light of understanding can shine on all you have previously learned— all that you already embody. All of the wisdom, from the books that you have read and the teachers that you have heard, begins to glow. All of your knowledge starts to come to the forefront of your being. True sense arises not just through conscious Awareness, but also through bodily intelligence. Without neurotic clinging or pulling, you begin Awakening to the body's own temple of wisdom.

YOUR CHANGES
WILL BE CUMULATIVE

Living Ecstasy is the Tao coursing through every cell, coursing through every breath, coursing through every function, coursing through every organ of your body. Living Ecstasy in the body is your inheritance and it is your only real legacy. Like all of the other portals to Living Ecstasy that you have been shown, this one is right here, right now, available in this moment, never to be lost, never to be hidden, always available and always accessible. Living Ecstasy Itself is happy to serve you in this, your temple-body.

Know that the body you have received is the Universe's gift of utter perfection to you. The Universe is singing, "Look Precious One; here is your form, to dance the cosmos with, to dance your relationships with, to dance this heroic journey of Life. Here is the vehicle to use experience all things and to use to Bless all beings." You do not *have* the key. You *are* the key. And every time you use yourself to unlock Awakening in another it is remembered. Your own Awakening is cumulative. Whether you realize it or not, every time you step beyond your edge to offer yourself, you Awaken to what already is: Ecstasy."

Pain, pleasure, discomfort, ease, disease and health are all the very embodiment of what you are here to experience and to give away. You are spirit manifesting in the most auspicious way for you to learn in the highest way. You are you becoming more through your experiences in the body. What is gained through experience can never be taken away and in fact will be Blessed as wisdom once it is unselfishly offered through your open Heart for the sake of another. So, communicate in the most profound way; walk through the world in the most thoughtful way. Experience the pains and the pleasures of the body in the holiest way. This body is literally the temple embodiment of Living Ecstasy. Choose to care deeply and tenderly for you. To do so is to honor and to acknowledge with reverence the gift that is yours. To do so is to live in the rhythmic pulse of existence as an Ecstatic beacon of Love.

The Truth

Your body is the incarnation of Goodness.

— *nine* —

YOU ARE
WHAT YOU SEEK

"Now, consider the situation. You are
an unchanging and continuous being who
remains throughout all theses states that are
constantly changing and therefore transient.
But you are always there. It follows that
these fleeting objects are mere phenomena,
which appear on your being like pictures that
move across a screen. The screen does not
move when the picture moves. Similarly,
you do not move from where you are,
even when the body leaves home and
mixes in society.

Your body, the society, the forest,
and the ways are all in you; you are not in
them. You are the body also, but not this body
exclusively. If you remain as your pure self, the
body and its movements need not affect you.

what is bliss but your own being?
you are not apart from being which is the
same as bliss. you are now thinking that
you are the mind or the body which are
both changing and transient. but you are
unchanging and eternal. that is
what you should know...

can the feeling in this place be bliss?
when you leave here, you say you
are unhappy. therefore this peace is not
permanent; nay, it is mixed with unhappiness,
which is felt in another place. therefore,
you cannot find bliss in places and in periods
of time. it must be permanent in order that
it may be useful. such permanent being
is yourself. be the self that is bliss.
you are always that.

—Ramana Maharshi

ENJOY YOUR LAST MOMENTS
OF IGNORANCE

Love

Tenderness

Fun

Experience

Touch

Love

Safety

Abundance

Companionship

Power

Kindness

Knowledge

Joy

Fullness

Belonging

(fill-in-the-blank)

Challenge

Peace

Friendship

Opportunity

Success

Attention

Privacy

Adventure

Freedom

YOU
ARE
WHAT
YOU
SEEK.

You are seeking something outside of yourself.

You either do not realize that this is what you are doing, or you make up that this is what you must do. You are trying to fulfill a gaping hole, a painful gap of emptiness; a resounding hollowness that feels unfathomable and un-fill-able. Inside this void lives your inner troll who taunts you with feigned unworthiness and contrived lack to push you to keep looking outside of you to fulfill yourself.

You are driven by need or by desire.

You make decisions all day long from this place of lack and want. You become more and more separate from the fullness that you are. You become the **rat** in sep**a**rate. You squeeze down to a squealing, scampering version of your self, and you turn your Life into one big mission of finding and hording the goods.

You have it all backwards.

YOUR LIFE IS MEANT TO BE LIVED ANOTHER WAY.

There Is a Difference between Masculine & Feminine, Don't Panic

Every individual has a mix of Masculine and Feminine energies within them. The ratio varies from one person to another. Empirically it seems to be that most women have more of a Feminine essence while most men have more of a Masculine essence. The combination of these energies within each person is an immeasurable proportion.

> For the most part, it boils down to this: those who have a greater Feminine core mainly go through Life seeking Love, and those who have a greater masculine core mainly go through life seeking Freedom.

Some people who have more of a feminine essence try to fulfill their longing with a sense of Love, the *right* Love, the magical Love that will make nothing else in life really matter. When this Love comes, oh, they will finally be seen for who they really are.

When their hero Lover fails to appear or fails them in relationship, a more neurotic approach is pursued. The Feminine beast within is released and begins to shop, decorate, sex or eat in order to try to fill the black hole. The reason that this is neurotic is because, if you listen deep down, you already know that this hole is not fillable. Yet you want to feel Loved, so you go crazy trying to fill the unfillable hole. It is a sick part of the mind that tricks your adolescent self into remaining in this nutso pattern.

The Masculine part within you is simultaneously trying to get to emptiness. The Masculine seeks completion. There will be relief and release when you reach the finish line, when you get the job done, when you pay the bill, when you ejaculate or orgasm. AHHHH…those few precious moments of Freedom… The Masculine essence seeks

Freedom from all things in all things. There is an unending push to find some way for something outside of yourself to grant you the feeling of Freedom. You are always trying to seek emotional fulfillment through the ending of your mind and by the ending of your experiences. You try to reduce yourself to a place of simplicity, so that finally you will get some reprieve, so that your seeking, even for an instant, can come to an end.

The Masculine seeks to do the task or to take care of the thing that will end the stress and grant the heavenly ease of nothingness. "When the mortgage is paid, when my spouse is happy, when my finances are settled, when I have unburdened myself *then* I will be able to rest and to have ease and quietude." The neurotic impulse of the Masculine is to do whatever it can do, whether that is in real life or through video games, to reach the finish line of Freedom.

Seeking Strategies for Seekers

Seeking is crazy-making, yet you will do it until you burn out. So, right out of the gate, feel Free to take this advice: seek as much as you can for as long as you can. Seek power, seek money, seek sex, seek Love, seek shoes, seek victory…until you cannot help but seek the Truth. Because once you know the Truth, your seeking will never be the same.

Seek. Neurotically try to conquer in business; make a killing in the market or on a safari; settle down in a cabin in the snowy mountains; perform gargantuan acts of heroism. Seek smut. Seek satisfaction. Seek what is at the end of the rainbow. Seek nobility. Seek that unnameable quality that haunts you in your sleep again and again. Seek to end your stress, to empty your burdens and to lessen your load. Seek to Give for Giving's sake. Seek to Love for Love's sake. Seek to give meaning. Seek to find meaning. Seek to be meaningful.

If you fancy yourself a philosopher, endeavor to sit and think and talk of strategies that could be used to fulfill mans' wants and needs. If you are more of a historian, see how it is our ancestors successfully and unsuccessfully sought what they sought. Nobody knows better how to seek than extreme reverent religious followers of any faith. There are ranges of sophisticated to crude methods of seeking. You can seek through pure debauchery. You can meditate enough to empty your mind enough, so you can have a fleeting whisper of the True Freedom that You already Are. Seek to gorge and to fill yourself with every delight under the sun. Seek through clutter clearing, winning the lottery or falling in Love.

continued…

So, Guess What?!

You will seek to fulfill yourself. Then no matter what the level of fulfillment you experience, that troll inside of you will be doing its own chanting: "Do more so you'll have more, do more so you'll be more, be less so you need less; more, more, more, later, less, soon, need, want, deserve…"

The bizarre thing about any form of seeking is that you believe that this present attempt will create some future release into Freedom or some meaningful fulfillment of Love. Yet there only is this one moment and it is already perfect.

Your seeking is futile.

You already inherently possess all that can be sought.

Everything Is a Cycle Except for God

Aren't you old enough to know by now that this cycle of seeking is going to happen over and over again?

It is a temporary, repeated measure that gives you a short-time high followed by a long-term continuous arousing of the troll. Well, listen up to who and what is actually behind that troll. The troll and what it guards, that which you have been habitually trying to satisfy for eons, is none other than your spirit, none other than the spirit of Living Ecstasy, Itself.

The troll in the pit of your endless cycle of seeking is merely a mask of your own magnificence. It is You calling you back to God. It is whispering to you. Your own inner wisdom is saying, "Rather than seek Love and Freedom outside of yourself why not try *giving* the abundant Love and Freedom that You actually already Are."

change the inertia of the cycle.

From the tiresome emptiness of seeking to get, realize fulfillment by Giving.

change from seeking to giving.

Sure, at first you will simply be seeking to give, but that is the answer. You are here to Give Love and Freedom as the uniqueness that is You.

Gurus, spiritual teachings and Enlightened beings have been saying all of this through out the ages, so this is not new. And yet, it is important to hear. Hear it as if it is brand new. Finally pay attention to the brick that has been hitting your head. At last hear the walls that have been crashing down around you. But this time, don't run. This time don't look for shelter. Allow the hammer to hit you, and let the sky to fall.

A Secret

As long as you are caught in the insidious cycle of seeking, the actual flow of energy in your body runs in such a way that it keeps you dialed-in. You are kept like a drone, pre-programmed with patterns of feelings and behaviors that are actually not your own. The choice to give what you truly are causes your bodily energy patterns to reverse. You literally, bodily begin to feel more love and freedom the more you offer love and freedom.

YOU ARE *IT*

You are what you are seeking. The very thing you have been seeking is yourself. The way you have been seeking depends mostly on your makeup. The Masculine in you has been looking for Freedom because it has forgotten that Freedom is your own inner nature.

you are Love.
you are Love Loving itself
to, from and for others.

Really ask yourself what would happen if instead of trying to get Love, acceptance, attention, validation and approval from anyone outside of yourself, you started to give it all? Assume that You are the complete source of Love for this world. You are. Now, make choices from this knowledge. If you do not genuinely feel this to be so, then just do your best to offer Love especially whenever you don't want to. A miracle will touch your Life. Something Greater than you can expect will be yours. *It* already is Yours.

Sit in the Fire

You are already Free within. Instead of trying to find Freedom, make your decisions from that place. How would your Life be Lived if you absolutely knew that you are already absolutely Free? What if you Lived already Free? How would you LIVE right now knowing that you have the time, the resources and the energy it takes to experience everything you choose?

GOODBYE INNOCENCE

Go ahead and kiss not knowing goodbye. Here is a whopper: Life never will be conquered. You will never reach the magical state where everything is so perfect that you feel sustained Freedom and unending Love. Life will test and stress you no matter who you are.

TO LIVE AS BLISS, your True nature, you must choose IT.

Your soul is the canvas of Life. Your experiences, including your joys and your burdens, are the colors of eternity. You are the artist. You are The One who splashes the colors on the canvas. You are the Feedom to create. You are the Love that fulfills every dream. In Truth, you are it all. There is no need to focus on any one aspect giving it more importance than any other. Relax open. Relax open even in your closures. Relax open now.

> *You must choose Ecstasy again and again for as long as you are alive. Choose it and rest in that choice. Rest as Joy in all of the conditions that arise to makeup your Life.*

HELLO CHOICE

while intending to open
as Freedom and as Love,
Live your Life.

Begin each moment from the Free emptiness that is already behind every thought, feeling and experience. Fill each moment of Being with the complete fullness of Love that you certainly are.

Act from this place in your regular life. Ask, "What would Love do…How would Freedom behave?" Look everyone in the eyes. Show them the smile in you. Let them see the Truth through your humorous disposition, through your empathetic offerings and through your patient playfulness. Choose to be bright. By being happy with who they are, show others that they need nothing else in the world outside of themselves. Love everyway another shows up. By offering Love and Freedom when you do not feel like it, or when they do not deserve it, you transmit that they are what they seek. By relaxing your neurotic requests and demands of others, you give them the space to be the Freedom that they are. Your own neuroses will also increasingly relax. The extraordinary result is that Living Ecstasy will start to take root within you more and more.

Love is what Living Ecstasy feels like. Love is what God feels like. Light is what God looks like. And Emptiness is that Freedom which God is appearing in.

Know that every form of connection and space is your very self. It is not a far away state, something to be achieved nor a roller coaster of emotions. You need not be a slave to the ups and downs of the every day highs and lows of Life. Love and Freedom is your Truth. Breathe, move and bloom, knowing the Truth. Allow your depth to shine as the art of your Life.

Rest your efforts, precious One,
you are complete.

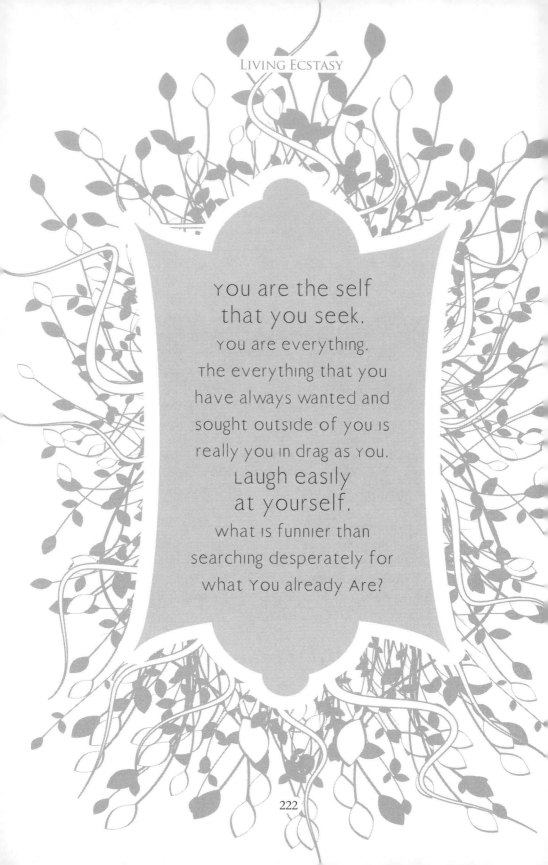

You are the self
that you seek.
You are everything.
The everything that you
have always wanted and
sought outside of you is
really you in drag as You.
Laugh easily
at yourself.
what is funnier than
searching desperately for
what You already Are?

— ten —

EVERYONE'S ENLIGHTENMENT DEPENDS ON ME

"we're studying dharma, that is, how things actually are. Then, we try to live according to that...Between the unconscious, the subconscious, and the conscious mind, between your feelings and your body, your sensations and your emotional attitudes and your mental approaches to all these things, it's a wonder we ever get anything done in the way of growing spiritually. That is, coming into harmony with the way things are, living a dharmic life. This is not easy. It's hard. It will be necessary for you to accept help, guidance and love...

The most progress is made during the time that the least seems to be happening. It's the day-by-day doing of techniques, cultivating being kind to people, and applying the principles that make the progress...

You build up a habit of being kind to people... you start to yell back (at someone) and you think, "oh, why not just let it go?" and you do. That's the miracle. That's the test, but it's built in the fabric of having been kind repeatedly, day after day, week in and week out. That's the magic. There is no other magic unless it's your love for each other, but that love manifests through that routine activity...

Don't listen to your own mind trying to argue you out of it... practice... the reward for doing this is great. You will get peace, happiness and success, though not all in one day."

—charles Berner

TELL ME WHO YOU ARE

Who You Are, is not ultimately something to be discovered or to be Awakened to. Who You Are, is something that you are creating from moment to moment with the **intentions** of your thought-forms. A thought-form is a repeated recognizable thought that has formed into a pattern. You utilize these thought forms to build your world. A thought form seems to be solid and real, yet it only has the weight that you yourself give it. As you Awaken, you gain greater command over these thought-forms. You begin to understand how malleable reality actually is.

You literally begin to

create your own Awakening simply by realizing that you are indeed doing so.

True Awaking or Enlightenment can happen in a single moment-less moment. It is beyond the mind. You realize your absolute oneness with all that is. It is actual, yet it cannot possibly be explained. This direct experience is often followed by a euphoric honeymoon phase where you seemingly cannot shut up about it.

continued...

(CAUTION) You begin to proselytize your new Awareness to any and every one who is near you. When you startle from your slumber, you will recognize that the nature of being is emptiness. After the honeymoon fades, there will most likely be a stage where you will just sit in that emptiness and twiddle your thumbs with nirvana boredom. Eventually, you will begin to actively Awaken.

The active form of Awakening is a deep stirring to conscious Life. It is the moment when you finally really begin to Live. You know that you are the fullness and the source that is bursting with aliveness for everything and everyone around you. Such Awareness is the conscious manifestation in your mind, body and spirit of the precious path that you are actually meant to Live. You begin to actively wish to Live, so that you can offer. You do Awaken to give, to transmute and to transcend simultaneously again and again from moment to moment.

And so you create your reality in the sense that you are creating the self from moment to moment. That very self is being created within itself as well, and that, then, is a good place to begin, and it is a good place to die.

The self
is that which is

perceiving everything
inside itself

perceiving everything
within itself.

YOU CREATE YOUR REALITY: FACT OR CLICHÉ?

Manifestation is the tension between desiring and receiving. Whatever happens after desiring and before manifestation is the *how*, the way the manifestation occurs. You do not need to know anything about the how. You have a desire or an **intention**, and you simply offer it to the Universe, to God, to the Goddess, to the Divine, to Shakti. You offer your desire, and you let it go.

Suffering is a pastime. Some people enjoy that type of pastime. If you recognize that this very existence is Laila, meaning the play of the gods, then you will know that pain is what gives you a range of feeling. Pain is part of your palette. Pain is a particular viewing point of Bliss. **Suffering is a choice.** If you are going to do suffering, do it artfully. Do it in a way that uplifts all beings. Suffering that does not uplift all beings causes more suffering. So, make drama out of it. Make the blues out of it. Open wide as **exquisite suffering** itself for the sake of all beings everywhere.

Everyone's Enlightenment depends on me and on you and on anyone else you can think of. Taking on the responsibility, really tangibly, tacitly in your body for somebody else's Enlightenment, is the only significant thing you can do. Whatever you do in Life will dissolve. In fact, as soon as you can recognize an accomplishment it is disintegrating. It matters that you wake up from the delusion of the illusion. When you do, others will too.

Tell the Truth

What you do and how you share in order to evoke Truth between you and another is how genuinely you Live Truth and how profoundly Truth Lives you. When you intentionally take on the project of others' Enlightenment, you will not know *how* to do it. You will make a decision to do it. You will hold the **intention to do it above all else,** even above your own laziness and apathy. You will be ready to act when you intuit that the proper occasion has arisen. You will tell the Truth in your daily Life as best you can because to get to the big Truth you must start with the littler ones. And you will practice. Practice what is in this book. Practice what is in your own Heart.

Practice being bright, real and open.

What to Do?

When you allow this to sink in, and to be felt to its core, you will start breathing differently. You will actually begin breathing everyone else's tightness. You will feel intuitively where and how their constriction of Enlightenment is manifesting. Your own breath will start to feel those around you. You will breathe them deeper than you would breathe for yourself alone. Your posture will open. No matter what your mood, you will shine. You will be the conduit of the Free flow of Awareness of attention. You will be the beacon of Light and Love. Magic and Mystery will be more available to others through you and through them for you. The movement of your body will be a motion of dance and of Awakening. Your whole body will be as Shiva Itself doing the cosmic dance for all of creation. You will embody all the archetypes of all the great beings you have ever known. You will be the embodiment of Christ's Love. You will be Buddha's compassion.

THE TRICK TO GETTING WHAT YOU WANT

The key is to lift the eyes of your Heart up off of yourself to truly regard another. Then you will *see* that you are the Life Force of the Universe. You are the trees of nature recycling air, conscious and open. You are the soil giving nutrients and composting the dirt of Life. Awaken now so you can compost the suffering of another. Be touched. Be moved by the enormous awe of what you are. You are the fountain of youth. You are the wisdom of ages. You are the elixir to all that ails. Breathe in the darkness of another being and breathe out Light.

Enlightenment is not some fantasy New Age thinking or some fanciful altruistic way of being. It is a responsibility that you are accountable for. You are responsible for, not merely the Awakening and the Living Ecstasy of others, but for your very own self.

oh! what a day it will be when you know in your body, in your mind and in your Heart that there is no difference. Another is you, and you are another.

Get this: much of what you have been desiring to manifest has come from the limited smaller version of yourself that you have believed is really you. Align your wishes with the wide You and watch what happens. Authentically desire and **intend** something for the Awakening of another and watch the sparks fly.

it is so simple and so literal:
the more you give the more you get.

The Bottom Line

The trick to manifesting what you want is to come from the authentic brilliant Being that you really are.

YOUR MOOD AND YOUR MOTIVES DON'T MATTER

You might not like hearing this, but in order for you to begin, nothing has to change. You don't need more money or to become a better person. Any reason you can concoct to delay your active response of opening right now as the Light of the world, is a lie. You are the Light and the Life of the world. You don't need saving. You are the Gift.

Breathe the people around you.
When you are in a great mood, give it away.
When you are in a foul mood, open the other people
around you simply through the manifestation and
the magnification of your own magnificent
stinky openness. Give whatever you've got.
You know what to do, so for God's sake,
cut the crap, and do it.

What happens is jaw dropping. Those around you, by osmosis, start to Awaken. Those around you start to have their darkness rise to the top to be seen. As your Light shines onto their darkness, their darkness is lifted and brought to the surface. In that moment, when they begin spewing spite and ire, breathe it all in even deeper. Allow yourself to be totally transparent to them.

EVERYTHING IS ATTRACTED
TO THE LIGHT

What to Do?

Allow yourself to be transparent to everyone and everything.
Show your positive aspects, your neutral aspects and above
all show your dark aspects. Openly display the parts of you
that you would rather not disclose to others, you would rather
not face yourself and you would rather not experience at all.
Show yours and see theirs. Let it all penetrate your Heart.
With every inhalation become a vessel of purification for
those around you. With every exhalation let it all pass out of
you, purified by the fire of Love. Become the cleansing for those
you care about and ultimately for those you do not care about.
The brighter you shine, the more muck will be drawn to you
and the more you will be able to offer your Grace.

Ultimately, you will face a reckoning with those for whom you have any form of resistance. Whether they be tainted political leaders, selfish power-mongers or dastardly deeds culprits, the solution is for you not to let any separation hold you back from allowing and enabling them to Awaken. This is not just a lesson or a process, this is a sacrifice. It is not a noble sacrifice, but it is the only sacrifice. Either you are Aware of it or you are not, but it is your single aim, your only goal. Awaken to be The One who is liberating all other beings by your own example and by your own shining Light. Show the way by granting Freedom and by offering Love. Do it steadily as if it is your purpose for Living. Do it without fanfare as though you are Truth's under-cover agent.

Shine, Shine, Shine

When you come to the place where you have achieved so much in your Life that your well of fulfillment runneth over, that is when you naturally become The One who is Living Awakening. Enlightenment can happen any which way. You may directly experience the moment-less moment of revelation and awe, or you may slowly blossom into the Great knowledge over the course of time. Here is a tip: how you wake up doesn't matter a bit. What matters is what happens after your own Awakening has begun. What you do after the bang or the bloom is what your legacy is. All you need to do for yourself, for others, for your Mom, for your country, for Goodness' sake is to shine your Heart. Shine it. Shine it big. And surrender to where this takes you.

So, allow your cup to runneth over. Allow yourself to be Unreasonably Happy. Your Enlightenment, everyone's Enlightenment depends on you. Let each being who reads this take on that ultimate, profound surrender, that vital profound activity, that definitive profound Love offering. Use your body, your breath, your career, your lifestyle, not just for yourself. Continually sacrifice your smallness to the Divine on behalf of all.

The First Nations People have an ancient tradition. Their teachings instruct them to let every action they do and every choice they make come from the most **intentional** place within. The old ways guide them to act with depth of clarity. They consider how their actions will impact the future seven generations of humanity across the entire world. They practice feeling into the impact of their actions and choices in all directions through time and space.

Sit in the Fire

To take such an approach, requires deep solemn sanctity and vast Heartfelt vulnerability. This effort is a humanness that is tapped from the core of the Divinity within. It is not a practice of transcendence from where you are now into other realms. It is a wise practice of fully descending into your human-ness. To do so requires extraordinary depth of empathy. You must feel bereavement. You must open to the genuine suffering of others. You must let go to know total elation. You must be consciously will-ing to feel the whole gamut of the human experience while remaining sensitive, vulnerable, unified, open and caring. From such sober **intention**, the way you create your Life through your choices will naturally, profoundly and practically unfold in a way that cannot help but bring Enlightenment for others. Such shine will permeate your every breath, your every action, your every step, and ultimately your every thought. Amen.

You Are Seen

Enlightenment is the magnificent Mystery which will cleverly hold Itself behind a veil until you discover It for yourself. Enlightenment is the Secret of Secrets. Enlightenment is waiting for you to find It, to claim It, to Live It and to give It away. Enlightenment is Living Ecstasy laid totally naked. It is your brightly bejeweled cloak. Once you don this magical garment it will melt into your being to reveal your own True colors. Enlightenment is the illumination of the Truth, without any projection, pouring out as Light from you. Enlightenment is Living Ecstasy.

Enlightenment is your True beauty, undressed, relaxed and released.

As you read these words, be released from any ignorance or bondage and from any idealism or patterns that have kept you bound in smallness or in misery. Enlightenment is something that can only be experienced, yet It is not an experience. Once it is known to you, it can be stabilized through your practice of the Living Ecstasy principles. Practice is what will always bring you back to the authentic natural way of Being.

Recall a moment of sweetness, excitement or Bliss in your Life. Perhaps it is when your Grandmother held you, when you first fell in Love, when you first saw your baby or when you laughed so hard your sides ached. Really put yourself in that experience. Allow yourself to fully feel now what you felt then. Now with your imagination, animate and exaggerate that moment. Intensify the joy and stretch the length of that moment until it fills every cell in your body and spills out to fill the room. Imagine that moment exploding with such joyous force that it is all you can feel. Really let the happiness of that moment touch you. Now, even if you really let yourself experience this—no matter how grand it is—it is still just a tiny bit compared to the staggering Knowledge and Ecstasy of Enlightenment. Enlightenment is Ecstasy. It is real, and It is yours.

You can choose right now to Live your Life as an Enlightened Being. Intuitively you know how. Here in these pages you are also shown many ways how. What happens when you choose to Live Enlightened, is that you stabilize as the embodiment of Living Ecstasy. You come Home, not through the mind, not through scripture and not through sacrifice, but by your own choice you walk through Life as a wide open, conscious being. Actual Enlightenment is what you will become after your choice to rip away the veil and your continual decision to practice. You are seen. Rise up and take your place.

You are seen by Love.

For the Sake of Others,
You First

You have to focus on yourself first; it is important to be able to solidify your own spine of consciousness and to open your own Heart. All of your closures are actually an active choice that you undertake. At first, you will feel like it is your choice to open again and again. Eventually you will begin to see that the real choice you have been making all along is to close. When you are able to see the patterns of how you consciously close, you will notice that other parts of you are being nourished. For example, you will naturally have increased magnetism, power, abundance and FUN.

To become Aware of your closure, you must become more spiritually supple. Through our own personal practice, meditation, self-discovery and reflection from good friends, you will start to recognize that your closure actually has nothing to do with circumstances, others or your own history. Your closure is a result of the momentum of your incarnation. In effect it is arbitrary. It really need not concern you. Your responsibility is to practice openness. Eventually your practice will undo itself or run its course, and you will simply Be What You Are.

Within you now there is always that little spark and glimmer of the wink going on. The part of you that is so purely conscious that It can never be snuffed out or diminnished. It is the eternal spark of knowledge of what is really happening. The Love that sustains Existence flows through You. When you are able to see the games that you play then you are able to relax those games. You can allow yourself to laugh more and to Live fuller. You will start to see what is manifesting in others. You won't be able to help it. The deeper you get to know yourself the deeper you will automatically know others. The more clearly you understand your own traps, greed, aberrations and sneakiness, the more empathetic you become to others and the better your relationships will be.

You start to wake up from your tiresome game of hide and seek.

instead of hide and seek you become found and seen.

You become more sensitive, alive and Aware.

continued...

This is your official
wake-up call.

Do not worry about your preferences,
your problems, your circumstances or
your ego. Just take responsibility
for the statement:

Everyone's enlightenment
depends on me.

And, see what happens.
That's it!

Just take it on as best
you can, and the rest
will take care of itself.

— eleven —

MAY ALL BEINGS DRINK FROM THIS WELL OF UNREASONABLE HAPPINESS

You are a non-physical consciousness that is
experiencing physical reality.

You were created in the image of
the creator, your essential essence is
unconditional love and the experience
of ecstasy is your birthright.

You are here on Earth at this time
because you chose to be.

The highest purpose of your life is to be
yourself to the best of your ability and live
each moment as fully as possible.

You always have free will and the freedom to choose.

Anything you can imagine is possible
for you to experience.

You attract your life experiences through
the interaction of your strongest beliefs,
emotions and actions.

Excitement is the physical translation of the
vibrational resonance that is your true, core
natural being. Follow your excitement!

You are naturally abundant and your choices
are always supported by Creation.

There are only four laws in creation:

1. You exist.
2. The One is All and the All are One.
3. What you put out is what you get back.
4. Change is the only constant... except for the first three laws, which never change.

There is actually only one moment in Creation. Everything you experience is the same moment from a different point of view.

You create the past and the future from the here and now.

You are an eternal being and while you may change your form, you cannot cease to exist.

Everything you experience is another aspect of yourself.

You are loved so unconditionally by Creation that you can even choose to believe that you are not loved.

—Bashar

DRINK UP

Unreasonable Happiness is the happiness that arises when there are no restrictions over your soul or over your Heart. Unreasonable Happiness is your birthright. That means it inherently is yours. You more than deserve it. You fundamentally possess it. You are it. Unreasonable Happiness is the fruit of your practice.

The deeper, the more intentional, the more Heartfelt and the more surrendered your practice becomes, the more you will walk in genuine sweetness and sublime grace.

Your practice is you dipping into the well again and again to Freely drink the elixir of Life. Your practice will bring you to maturity. You will be able to Live more easily because you will be able to see the humor that lurks behind every drama.

Sit in the Fire

Q: What do you want?

A: Unreasonable Happiness.

Q: What are you?

A: Unreasonable Happiness.

Q: What is Unreasonable Happiness?

A: You.

It is the equation of Life.

It is the only solution and the final outcome.

Unreasonable Happiness is the question and the answer.

The guaranteed outcome of conscientiously following the principles of Living Ecstasy as best you can moment to moment is a Life stabilized in Unreasonable Happiness. Remember you do not need to change your state. You do not need to whip yourself up into a feel good, pumped up, workshop seminar frenetic craziness. You do not need to first remedy any challenge you are facing. In fact, as you diligently practice Living Ecstasy, the desire for remedies will start to naturally dissipate.

Do you see the paradox? When you enter a situation that has you facing closure, stress or fear, and you open and offer Unreasonable Happiness Itself, then what you gain is Joy, Peace and Prosperity. You have to give whatever it is you wish to gain. The solution to every paradox and to every riddle is Unreasonable Happiness. When you make being Unreasonably Happy the foundational choice of your existence, the inevitable outcome is immeasurable abundance. When you want to close, take and horde, then it is time to open, give and share.

Unreasonable Happiness means that you are happy without a reason. You do not have to explain why you are so happy to anybody. Why are you happy? How come you are smiling? What is making you laugh? What do you feel so good about? You do not have to answer that. There is no answer. Unreasonable Happiness is without any cause, motive or explanation. It is Happiness happening simply because YOU ARE.

You Can't Fake Happiness

War, poverty, anger, injustice, illness, calamity…These things are not going to go away.

you cannot fix anything because
nothing,
INCLUDING YOU,
is broken.

The nature of Life contains horror, evil and misfortune. Your job is to say, "Those things are happening, *and I am Unreasonably Happy.*" The darker it gets, the more you authentically shine as real Freedom and glory. Be the first to Love. Do not complain. Let gratitude Light your way. Put your attention on what is Good, and cling to that as you weather the storms.

Unreasonable Happiness is the base of your pyramid. A pyramid stands the test of time. Its base is wide and strong. It is built solid, so it can hold everything else on top. Once you have faith in the strength of your foundation, once you discover for yourself that your base is Bliss, you will Live the Life of God's design.

If you put your attention on Love, you will magnify Love. When a challenge arises in your Life, do not resist or ignore it. Do not simply put on a fake glossy happiness over the top of what is really going on. Breathe. Feel as deeply as you can all aspects of the event and the emotions it stirs. Breathe. Choose. Choose to open Truthfully as whatever is unfolding. Feel it openly on behalf of others. Find the Wink. Intuit what exists behind and underneath the pain, fear or unpleasantness. Decide to come from that place in the middle of dilemma. Stand strong knowing that *any moment now…*

The Truth

You will increasingly experience what you naturally give away: Peace, play, empathy, abundance, excitement and Love. You will progressively know and emanate the Truth, we are all one; we are all safe; we all are Free; and we all are Loved. Where you put your attention will more and more match your **intention**, which will inevitably become that all people in all conditions know that they are the Heart.

The Power of Yearning

"All beings, drink from this well of Unreasonable Happiness." This is the joyous cry of your own Unreasonable Happiness yearning for everyone else around you to wake up. It is a shout that declares that it is time to wake up to what we all actually are, what we can be and what we will be. May all beings Live as Unreasonable Happiness is the intention that Joy, Love and Freedom profoundly reign supreme as our outward display of Life and relationship. May Ecstasy benefit and nourish each soul. Drink. Drink from this well. Live your own unique way. May all Beings drink from this well. You be the thirst-quenching angel of mercy. You be the little lepricon of luck. You be the sage of wisdom. And may all Beings drink from YOU.

Yearning is very powerful. Let your yearning be your prayer for yourself and for others. Genuine yearning creates movement; it creates a crack in what seems solid. Through this crack Love and Light can pour through. Then the crack can widen. Yearn deeply. Yearn sweetly. Yearn for Blessings, and Bless with your Yearning.

What to Do?

When you want to act, but you do not know what to do, breathe. As you breathe and open, Bless and yearn. These are powerful forces that create change. Be ready to demonstrate patience, surrender and trust. Remember, you will not know *how* things will unfold, and it is a waste to fret over the how. Yearn, breathe and wait. Bless, breathe and give.

THE BOTTOMLESS WELL

What to Do?

You want to heal the past? Live now as Unreasonable Happiness. You want a bright future. Live now as Living Ecstasy. You want a better world. Outwardly offer what you are inwardly made of. Pretty soon you will discover that there is no inside or outside of anything. There is only your grateful, humble offering in this very moment. Drink and welcome others to drink from the infinite spring of Unreasonable Happiness.

YOur Happiness already exists
before you wake up in the morning
and your feet touch the floor.

This is True literally and figuratively. Real Happiness precedes Life. Real Ecstasy is not the result of anything. You are already Unreasonably Happy, Happy without reason. Whether it is waking up in the morning or waking up in Life, the Truth of you is that you are already Bliss. Any other condition is something that you are actually actively doing over the top of this center. To access this Truth is simple. Wake up, breathe and feel all the way out, and at the same time breathe and feel all the way in. The non-existent place where the two of these meet is your limitless core of Living Ecstasy. The well can never run dry because it is the source of all things, and the condition of all things is Ecstasy.

Decide and declare that you are Living your Life from this place. It is an inward declaration that spreads outward in all directions through space and time.

EVERYTHING AROUND YOU IS TRYING TO SHOW YOU

When you are not drinking from the well of Unreasonable Happiness, what are you doing? Why are you doing that? Look around. Pick something, anything around you. It can be a rock, a wall, the refrigerator, your friend, a situation, a problem…anything. Put your attention on whatever you have chosen, and open to it. Do this until you touch Ecstasy, and Ecstasy touches you. There, you just drank from the well of Unreasonable Happiness. If it takes you a while, so what? This is Ecstasy you are dealing with. It is worth a little discipline on your part.

There is indeed a world-wide conspiracy going on. You are involved. Everything is in cahoots. Everything is made of the same thing, and it is all conspiring on your behalf. Every particle of everything is showing you, luring you, tricking you—whatever it takes—to bring you back to God. Come Home, dear One, rest in this moment, you are Home. There is nowhere to go, there is nothing to do. Drink from the well.

Let laughter be the zen stick you slap on your shoulder. Let kindness be your tithe. Let patience be your devotion. Let yearning be your dance. Let love be your altar.

Do it all, not to be seen, but rather to see. Offer it all, so that every parched soul you encounter will find a place to quench their suffering and to replenish their spirit.

A Secret

Everything around you is a reminder of God. Everything around you is inviting you back Home to Bliss.

LOOK.

Look, and be willing to really see. Nothing is actually still. Everything is in Ecstatic dance for you.

THROW A PARTY AND GET DRUNK

There is a party going on, alright. The Mystery provides the party hall that is decorated with every emotion that has ever been felt. God is the DJ playing the songs that soul provides. The guests arrive full in fancy costumes that they picked out themselves. Closure provides the entertainment. You, of course, are the host. Sometimes you are so caught up in it all that you temporarily forget your only duty which is to pass out the punch. But you always eventually snap back, and when you do, the party is really on.

Give lavishly. You have been drunk on Joy before. There is nothing else like it. May all Beings drink from this well of Unreasonable Happiness until they are so drunk that they forget themselves. They forget that they are nasty, selfish, hurtful and small. Anything can happen at a party. You are the Life of the party. Drink past all of your limitations. Be extravagant as you pass the cup to others.

> *May all beings drink from this well of Unreasonable Happiness until they are so drunk on Bliss that they remember who they are. They remember that they are gentle, strong, wise and Free.*

GET THAT IT IS A PRACTICE

Unreasonable Happiness is a practice. Your ego will try to find some way to outsmart this or to get around it. You see, the ego is not a thing. It is not some monster munchkin sitting around in the control room of YOU, planning to run and ruin your life. The ego is an on-going action. It is a part of you just the same as your liver is a part of you. You do not need to conquer the ego any more than you need to conquer your organs. You do not need to fix or focus on your ego. You *do* need to practice.

All the events in our Life, positive and negative, bring you tension. It does not matter what it is, it is covering the deeper You. Every event is a distraction from Bliss unless you make it an event of Bliss. Consider that Bliss is your covert and overt mission. Nothing that happens is to be discarded. Rather all is to be felt into for its root. At the root you will find Ecstasy. If you don't, it is because you have not dug deeply enough, you have not felt deeply enough.

practice

Be unwavering in your purpose to reveal the Ecstasy in *all* things, in all people, in all emotions, in all places and in all events. This is practice. Breathe. This is practice. Open. This is practice.

Above all, your practice is to keep practicing! Do your best. Your best is *enough*. Open your eyes to those around you. Realize that they are doing their best. Cease to blame others or to beat yourself up. To do so is a giant waste of your Life force. You can use that same energy to dip back into the well. Unreasonable Happiness means that you take care of yourself and others in every way possible. Practice is your map to the well. The more you practice the more lit the path becomes. The well is for every sacred Being. And every Being is sacred.

— epilogue —

THE BEGINNING:
BE UNREASONABLY HAPPY

What is the secret to living a happy life?
Keep on doing it, and keep on doing it!

What does "the Wink" mean?
There is a plug and a cord attached
to every single person.
It's like a tree.
All the branches are people.
No matter what, they are all connected.
When a branch falls off, it's the cord of anger.
The roots connect every single person.
Everything in this world is connected.

What does it mean to "fill the room with who you are"?
Fill up the room with Love.
Fill it up.
Open your heart and let it all out ~
all the Love ~ never anger.
Breathe in all the good stuff.

What is your advice for all the people reading your Dad's book?
Read the book and take it all in.
You don't have to take all our advice.
Take it all in, and take out what you don't like.

— Shaman Raja, age 8

Dear Loved One, you cannot fail. You are not wrong. Gently and firmly set down your shame. Step away from the cage. The door has always been open. You are a treasure. Your purpose is to be you. Nothing needs to be fixed. The fastest way through your suffering is to feel it, and then to offer to someone else whatever it is that you yourself are so desperately desiring. Let your Heart SHINE like the sun.

Feel before the beginning and beyond the end of any crisis, predicament or unfolding. That part of you is Home. Welcome. That part of you is unfettered and cannot be touched by the fluctuations that occur on the surface of your Life. Rest. Sink and surrender as openness. Laugh more, especially at yourself. This is the most practical thing to do, and yet it is the most vulnerable. Allow yourself to Be absolutely permeable to the very things you fear. Emerge, wake up and transcend all pain and pettiness. Eventually you will discover this book to be True. So, choose now to drink deeply from the well of Unreasonable Happiness. Miracles of Prosperity are abundantly yours. You do not need to earn or to change anything.

open your Heart as You Are to what is.
shine as the beacon of Light that You Are.
shower everyone with your Love,
Laughter and Freedom.

YOU are cut from the
cloth of the one HEART.

Accept things as they are.
seek to see the
True nature of things.
Everything includes you and
you are included in everything.
Your experiences and emotions
are not you. You are indefinable.

Be real. Be simple.
Be kind.

No matter how low you feel
or how bleak things seem,
when you start to give, it will all
change. You can count on change.

Every possibility
is yours.

The secret is You.

You are Living Ecstasy.

"Every one of us desires to **Be Awake**. Every one of us desires to Live from **deeper authenticity**. We all want to be more REAL as well as to have relationships that are more REAL."

—*Satyen Raja*

 ## SPECIAL ECSTATIC OFFER!

As a **THANK YOU**, for purchasing *Living Ecstasy* www.LivingEcstasyBook.com, **Satyen Raja** is offering a **scholarship** for you and a family member to attend our famous, internationally renowned, **WarriorSage 5 day Illumination Intensive** as complimentary guests.

This is truly an incredible **gift**, valued at $5,994.00 for two. The Illumination Intensive is for people who want to Live with more **Truth** in their Life, more authenticity! Are you ready to break through your barriers and let the REAL **YOU** *emerge*? This is for you!

At the Illumination Intensive:

✓ You will Find *your own* deepest, Truth, Wisdom and Authenticity!
✓ You will EMPOWER your deepest spiritual convictions as you journey along the path of Enlightenment, Free from dogma and doctrine!
✓ You will cultivate amazing Communication Skills so you can fully Express what is truly in *Your Heart*!!
✓ You will CONNECT to a Deep Peace that you can bring into your *daily* Life—even under the most challenging situations.
✓ You will enter an Infinite place within you, so you can Manifest all of your deepest Heart's desires.
✓ You will CLEAR weighty barriers, patterns and beliefs so you can Live your Life with Truth, Fulfillment and Purpose.

continued...

What People are saying about the Illumination Intensive...

"I highly recommend Satyen Raja's teachings to anyone truly interested in transforming their lives..."

I recently attended the WarriorSage five day **Illumination Intensive**. Words fail to make the desired impact when I say these courses created dramatic and instant change in my life. **I was seeing "miracles" occur** that I couldn't explain, and I truly felt that I'd done **"work"** on unseen levels of my being. I highly recommend Satyen Raja's teachings to anyone truly interested in **transforming their lives**.

Nicole Whitney, Producer/Host
News for the Soul & Life Changing TV

"I found what I spent my entire life looking for..."

I can't use words to describe what has happened... I feel like I have been **blown wide open**... I get *me*. I found what I spent my entire life looking for, and for that *I'm profoundly grateful*.

Amanda van Merlin

" I was sick of living a half life..."

I was sick of living a half life, of making do, of getting by. Deep inside, I knew my life had to be more than pretense and hidden desperation. The **Illumination Intensive** provided the sacred space, like a midwife at a birth, I was guided, encouraged, coached, teased and loved to bring **my deepest truth into the present**. The truth I discovered is that I am a magnificent being, surrounded by magnificent beings because **we are all magnificent**. I find myself falling in love with every person I meet, simply admiring and loving who they are. Life is truly a warm fulfilling adventure.

Egbert de Haan

THE GIFT OF ENLIGHTENMENT

You have just been given one of the most precious gifts that anyone could ever give you!

FREE TUITION FOR TWO
Valued at $5,994.00 to attend…

The Illumination Intensive 5 Day Workshop!

When you attend this talked about seminar, you can discover Who You Are…and how you can Live in your deepest Truth.

To register and for more information go to
www.LivingEcstasy.com
or call ☎ 1-800-815-1545
toll-free or ☎ (604) 534-0616

Space is limited, so register now!

This extraordinary free scholarship is valid only for people who have never attended a WarriorSage Illumination Intensive, and it is limited to your tuition. You are responsible for your meals and accommodation.

**** This offer is open to all purchasers of Living Ecstasy who have not yet taken an Illumination Intensive; First timers only. The value of this free admission for you and a companion is worth $5994.00. While participants will be responsible for their travel, meals and accommodations, Tuition to the program is complimentary. Participants in the training are under no financial obligation whatsoever to WarriorSage Training or to Satyen Raja. WarriorSage reserves the right to refuse admission to the Illumination Event if WarriorSage believes it will be conducive to the overall success of the event. ****

Experience the
Living Ecstasy Ebook
and share the journey
with friends and family at

www.LivingEcstasyEbook.com